Books by M. Blaine Smith

REACH BEYOND YOUR GRASP: Embracing Dreams That Reflect God's Best for You—And Achieving Them

MARRY A FRIEND: Finding Someone to Marry Who Is Truly Right for You

THE YES ANXIETY: Taming the Fear of Commitment

OVERCOMING SHYNESS: Conquering Your Social Fears

ONE OF A KIND: A Biblical View of Self-Acceptance

FAITH AND OPTIMISM: Positive Expectation in the Christian Life

KNOWING GOD'S WILL: Finding Guidance for Personal Decisions

SHOULD I GET MARRIED?

EMOTIONAL INTELLIGENCE FOR THE CHRISTIAN

Emotional Intelligence

for the
Christian

❑ *How It Radically Affects Your Happiness, Health, Success, and Effectiveness for Christ*

❑ *How to Achieve It Where It Counts Most*

M. Blaine Smith

SilverCrest
B•O•O•K•S

© 2012 M. Blaine Smith

SilverCrest Books
P.O. Box 448
Damascus, Maryland 20872

e-mail: scr@nehemiahministries.com
www.nehemiahministries.com

Library of Congress Control Number: 2012917856

ISBN: 978-0-9840322-6-6

I

The Radical Difference
Self-Understanding
Makes

1

Growing Wise
Emotionally

THE MOVIE *A BEAUTIFUL MIND* documents John Forbes Nash, Jr.'s battle with mental illness. The Princeton mathematician suffered from schizophrenia most of his adult life. The film stunningly portrays how Nash learned to question the reality of illusory persons, who appeared to him often, and seemed as real to him as the waiter who served you breakfast at the coffee shop this morning, or the friend who paid you a visit at home last evening. Just as important, he learned to deny their predictions of doom, and refused to accept their guidance as valid for his life.

Most impressive is that Nash lived an increasingly productive life as the years wore on. His crowning experience came in 1994 when he was awarded the Nobel Prize in economics.

Nash's odyssey with schizophrenia demonstrates that it's

possible to gain greater control over a debilitating psychological problem than we might imagine. His example gives hope to anyone suffering from serious mental illness, that there may be even brilliant light at the end of that horribly dark tunnel.

His example is deeply encouraging to the rest of us as well. Most of us don't face the sort of psychological challenges Nash did. We don't have to question whether the person standing in front of us or the furnishings in the room around us are mental holograms. We may assume that the reality our eyes see and our ears hear *is* reality.

Yet the reality that our *mind* assumes to be true—or quite possible—can be another matter altogether.

We may suffer fears that bear little relation to the truth, yet are still effective in shutting us down and holding us back from taking steps with our life that would succeed. We may be tortured by second thoughts in a decision, even though we've thought it through carefully and have substantial reason to move forward. Or we may be too quick to think we'll be better off caving in to anger and expressing it unkindly to someone. And the anger we feel may spring from assumptions that are terribly inaccurate.

The perceptions we fall into in such areas can limit us just as greatly as psychotic delusions did in Nash's case. Our challenge is also similar to his in important respects. We have to come to grips with the ways our mind is capable of misleading us, then make our best effort at these points to separate fact from illusion. The fact that Nash was able to gain mastery over the demons of schizophrenia is tremendously reassuring, and gives us hope that we can successfully wage our own battles of the mind—which are typically less formidable than his.

What John Nash's example shows us, more than anything else, is the value of gaining psychological self-awareness. For him, it made all the difference in finding the path to a productive and fulfilling life. Each of us will also benefit remarkably from gaining a clearer understanding of our own temperament, and of how we need to filter its impressions.

Meeting Life's Psychological Challenges

In his ground-breaking book *Emotional Intelligence,* Daniel Goleman stresses that we have a chronic need for such self-understanding.[1] He notes that we humans are easily led astray by our feelings, which often distort our thinking. Our emotions can take over our rational process so totally that our view of reality is drastically skewed—a problem Goleman terms "emotional hijacking."

The driver stewing with road rage, for instance, is musing, "To maintain any integrity, I have to teach that idiot who cut me off a lesson he'll never forget. I'll drive so close to the side of his car that he thinks I'm going to hit it." In a calmer moment the offended driver would never imagine such action would be cathartic. Yet as his anger explodes, he quickly spins into crazed logic. He now sees sideswiping the other's car as his personal mission. In this case his emotions have fully hijacked him.

In less extreme cases our emotions mislead us more subtly. Yet they can still be potently effective in swaying us to bad judgment. An important part of maturing, Goleman explains, is learning to manage our emotional process so that it works *for* us and not against us. We need a keen understanding of how we are wired, and why our feelings flow in certain ways under certain circumstances. Awareness of how we function psychologically removes the element of surprise, making it less likely our feelings will sabotage us.

We also need to make many adjustments for our particular psychological tendencies. Learning not to fan the flame of anger or nurture unhealthy fear is important. It's essential, too, not to let ourselves get so overstressed that we're susceptible to emotional hijacking.

Just as crucial, we need to learn to question perceptions influenced by runaway emotions, and refuse to let them be our final take on reality. We should take our emotional state strongly into account in all our decisions, and filter out assumptions induced too readily by anger, fear, or distraught feelings.

At the same time, we greatly need the constructive energy our emotions provide. A major part of our task is learning how to best open ourselves to the influence of positive feelings, such as love, empathy, hope, and natural motivation for certain work.

These are some of the steps necessary to develop emotional intelligence. We need it every bit as much as academic knowledge, Goleman insists. Unfortunately, our educational system gives scant attention to helping us grow smarter psychologically. It turns out many people who are brilliant in their fields of knowledge, but can't handle their feelings well.

Goleman is strongly on target. If we are to successfully move through life—to live productively, to accomplish our dreams, to make meaningful contributions to others' lives—we need emotional intelligence as much as any other skill or personal quality. We need to become good psychological thinkers, and able to manage our own psyche well. Knowing what to expect from our emotions, how to compensate for them, and how to draw maximum strength from them, enhances our potential considerably in every area of life.

The Christian and Emotional Intelligence

The goal of growing wiser emotionally is an important one for us as Christians, and would seem to fit naturally with our need to become more Christlike. Unfortunately, many Christians fall into a perspective about emotional life that hinders them. They assume that Christ expects them to give him control of their temperament, and that this is the end of the matter. This assumption is noble and well-intentioned. But what does it mean? That we should let Christ manage our emotions as though we were robots in his hands?

This is the sort of outcome we too often have in mind when we speak about having a "Christ-controlled temperament." We assume he will simply take over the whole emotional process for us, and relieve us of all struggle. Our role is to disregard negative emotions we experience and "give them up to him." We shouldn't give much attention to our desires and longings, either, which are likely to lead us down the primrose path; we should yield them to him, and assume that his will is probably different from what we naturally want.

God, though, is looking for a quite different response of obedience from us. His concern is that we learn to take responsibility, on all levels, for the life he has entrusted to us. This means becoming a good manager of our own emotional process. We should draw on his help and insight constantly as we do so; in that sense, we *are* giving him control. But if we expect him to do the work for us, we've missed the point. He wants us to take the same responsibility for growing emotionally that we do for growing intellectually.

We need, on the one hand, to develop a deep appreciation for the positive role our emotions play. Scripture stresses that they are a gift of God, providing the life-energy he uses to propel us in directions that reflect his will. When Paul declares that God "works" in us (Phil 2:13), the term he uses literally means "energizing." Paul is saying that God is stimulating us to take certain steps with our life. As we come to grips with what we are most motivated to do, we gain a treasured insight into how God has created us as individuals, and into what he wants us to do. Developing this self-understanding is the most thrilling part of emotional growth.

Our feelings may just as readily have a detrimental effect, and Scripture gives considerable attention to this side of it as well. Our emotions are an extraordinary force, like the wind, capable of driving us in both productive and unfortunate directions. Just as a sailor must respond to the wind by adjusting the sail properly, we need to interact with our emotions in a way that allows their energy to be life-giving and not destructive. The most challenging part of emotional growth is learning to deal with our emotions' contrary side.

The most difficult part of that challenge, moreover, is learning to think clearly at those times when our emotions have the potential to cloud our judgment. We need a healthy skepticism for the conclusions we reach then, and the astuteness to see reality for what it actually is. Knowing our vulnerable points, and being ready to make reality checks at such times, is vital.

Let's look more closely at what some of these instances typically are. These are some common occasions when we need to regularly question our conclusions, and refuse to let our emotions throw us off course:

1. Managing anger. No emotion colors our perception and clouds our judgment more quickly than anger. Our musings in the midst of it—about the person who has perturbed us, and about what action we suppose would be cathartic to take—are often gross distortions of the truth.

The most tragic assumption we fall into is that we will injure ourselves if we don't express the anger we feel. Ventilationist theories of the past century have stressed that we store anger. If not expressed, it builds up inside us and can cause us serious emotional or physical harm. In reality, though, we don't store anger any more than we store positive emotions. And expressing it just as often nurtures it as relieves it. Satisfaction comes not from expressing anger, but from resolving the problem that caused it.

We are rarely capable of addressing a problem constructively when our anger is at its height. It's a good rule of thumb to remember that our view of reality in a state of high anger is bound to be flawed. A valuable benchmark of our readiness to tackle a matter of contention is that we're finding ourself able to see things from the other person's viewpoint.

Reaching that point of empathy usually requires holding our tongue for the moment, taking some deep breaths, giving it some time, and perhaps a game of racquetball. We haven't grown fully wise emotionally until we instinctively question our assumptions of reality when we're angry, along with our need to immediately confront the other person. One of the surest signs of strong character is that we naturally put the brakes on the inclination to express anger unkindly. Gaining the ability to manage our anger this effectively should be a chief goal of emotional growth.

2. Guarding our heart. In this regard, we face an interesting dichotomy as Christians. Our desires provide us critical insight into how God has fashioned us, and thus into his will for our life. At the same time, our emotions lack discernment in themselves, and can fixate on objects of attraction that are anything but right for us. This leaves us with the ongoing challenge of distinguishing healthy desires from unhealthy ones.

Over time, our subconscious usually handles this task well, especially when we are in a growing relationship with Christ. Desires that have been with us for a long period and have stood the test of time are often excellent indications of God's guidance. Less seasoned desires have a greater potential to mislead us, and to prove Jeremiah's claim that the heart can be "deceitful above all things" (Jer 17:9).

An important part of growing wise emotionally is developing good judgment about our desires. We need clear perspective for determining which ones are constructive and which are not. Most important, we need to exercise this judgment often— choosing to nurture certain desires and not others. The married man who finds himself attracted to another woman, for instance, needs to avoid stoking that infatuation, as well as doing everything possible to rekindle his affection for his spouse.

The good news is that we do have considerable control over the long-term direction of our affections. With the right time and attention, our desires can become the life-giving motivational force God intends them to be.

3. Setbacks and major losses. Emotional pain, like physical pain, has the sense of forever to it. The most common reason teenagers commit suicide is heartbreak stemming from romantic rejection, and the belief they will never get over it and find it possible to love again.

Personal loss poses us two challenges. We have to believe that in time we'll have the opportunity to make a fresh start—that failure once doesn't mean failure forever. We also must believe we'll be *emotionally* able to let go of our hurt feelings and find a new outlet for our affection.

It's the latter conviction that's often the hardest to realize when we're reeling from a major loss. Yet in truth, God has made us remarkably resilient as humans. We can take the love we've felt for one person and redirect it toward another. We can take the passion we've devoted to one dream and reinvest it in another. Part of growing wise emotionally is learning that such refocusing of affection is possible, and bringing that fact to mind often when we're mourning an unhappy ending.

We usually need to allow ourselves some reasonable time to grieve a significant loss. Yet grief can become chronic. We need to make it a practice to question the perpetual sense of heartbreak we feel, and to remind ourselves constantly that it will pass—if we allow it to. And we need to open ourselves as fully as possible to the new beginnings Christ makes possible for us.

4. Paranoid assumptions. Most of us invest untold energy into worrying about what others think about us. When we look back on such ruminations, we so often find that they've hit wide of the mark of reality. It can be embarrassing to admit just how misplaced these concerns usually have been.

Most of us don't suffer from psychotic paranoia. Yet we do experience it often at a less extreme, but still stifling level. Our worries about what others think are inaccurate so much of the time, that we should assume by default they are wrong unless proven otherwise (especially since others are usually much less concerned about us than their own problems). We ought to make it a habit, whenever such suspicions set in, to tell ourselves there's high probability we're not thinking clearly.

We should see questioning our paranoid musings as part of our work in growing wise emotionally. This practice can relieve our anxieties significantly, and will likely improve our relationships with others as well.

5. Mood swings in decision making. Those of us with analytical temperaments usually find decision making difficult. A woman recently described to me her dilemma in deciding whether to marry her boyfriend: "When I'm up, I see all the reasons I should do it; when I'm down, I see all the reasons I shouldn't." Her emotional state affects her outlook so strongly that on one occasion she sees marrying this man as the opportunity of a lifetime, on another as the mistake of her life.

Those of us who suffer mood swings like this need to override the tendency, if we're to make firm commitments and realize God's best for our life. We should base our choices more on our pattern of feelings over time than on our emotions of the moment, and give more weight to the way we think when we're encouraged than when distressed or fatigued. Once we've diligently worked through a decision, we should stick with it— unless we encounter clear new information that gives us a strong reason not to proceed. Barring such new insight, we should regard doubts that surface when we're down as normal ruminations of our temperament, and not a valid take on reality.

"Don't doubt in the darkness what God has shown you in the light," as it's said. The adage is sometimes applied superficially to the Christian life. Yet it's sage wisdom when we've made a decision carefully and prayerfully, but then are dogged with second thoughts.

6. The need to rescue. There's another point where our emotions can mislead us, and, if we're not wary, beguile us considerably. Christ works within us who follow him to deepen our compassion for others. He builds into us a longing for our life to accomplish something of value to people, and calls us to do nothing less than give our life wholeheartedly to meeting others' needs.

Yet he calls us to *focus* in what we do for others as well, and to base our choices on the unique gifts, motivational pattern, and energy level he has given us. Each of us can only do so much, and none of us can be all things to all people (Paul's claim that he had become so, in 1 Corinthians 9:22, referred to his adopting customs of people he evangelized, not to his meeting every need he confronted).

Each of us faces many opportunities to help others, or to assist with worthy causes, where responding would stretch us beyond reasonable limits, and deplete the energy we need for commitments we've already made. Emergencies do occur, when we must draw on reserve energy and do our best to respond. But we cannot function effectively at the crisis level for long periods. Normally, God expects us to make careful choices about what we do to serve others, based on the capabilities he has given us. He wants us to live energetically, yet within our physical and psychological limits—to be good stewards of our life.

We are likely at times to feel the inclination to help—even a strong instinct to rescue—when it's not wise to respond. We should never assume that the impulse to help, in itself, is God's call to get involved, until we've carefully weighed all the relevant factors. We need, in short, to be big-hearted yet cautious in responding to others' needs, and the many opportunities to serve that come our way. Decisions to commit ourselves should be made as much with our mind as with our heart.

Making Emotional Intelligence a Habit

These six areas demonstrate the extraordinary importance of understanding both our temperament and our feelings at the moment, and taking these emotional factors strongly into account in our actions and decisions. Always, always, when we're inclined to act impulsively for any reason, we should stop and identify exactly why, and consider whether we're being driven to do something unwise that will come back to haunt us. Are my emotions hijacking me? Making a habit of asking the right questions makes all the difference—

(When angry:) Is anger clouding my judgment, and do I need to allow myself a chance to cool down before taking action? Am I on the verge of saying or doing something I'll soon regret and have to apologize for?

(When enticed:) Is craving overruling my better judgment at this moment, and masquerading as healthy desire? Am I about to do something that will end up damaging my health, reducing my effectiveness for Christ or hurting others?

(When reeling from a setback or loss:) Is there possibly a silver lining in what I've gone through? Is there something to learn that will help me be more successful in the future? Can I grow stronger through dealing with this reversal? Will God perhaps compensate by providing for me in another way? Can I remember a past time when a difficult loss paved the way for a great blessing? If so then, why not now?

(When obsessing about what someone thinks:) Do I have any clear evidence this person is thinking ill of me? Have such worries usually been wrong in the past? If so, isn't it likely they're off base now? Wouldn't I do better to expect the best from this individual? Might that expectation even prove to be a self-fulfilling prophecy?

(When feeling the need to rescue:) Does my urge to help this person or join this cause or take on this responsibility spring from my need to be a hero? Will saying yes in effect be saying no to other commitments I've already made, by robbing me of the time and energy to fulfill them? And have I honestly weighed how responding to this opportunity fits with my God-given gifts and the priorities to which Christ has called me? Should I rather pray for the grace to lovingly say no?

We not only should question our feelings when we're tempted to act from impulse, but also when we're hesitant to take a step that seems to make sense for us. Am I holding back due to fears that are probably exaggerated and wide of the truth? Is my vacillation simply inevitable, given my analytical temperament? Is it time to stop playing it so safe and to take a reasonable risk? Will I do better just to make my best choice, get on with it, and "let the chips fall"?

We should make a conscious practice of raising questions like these whenever our emotions are spinning out of control, and do so to the point that this self-prodding becomes a habit. As it grows routine for us, we've taken a big step toward managing our feelings well.

Daily Reflection

It also helps us greatly to spend some devoted time daily

reflecting on our emotional life—on how it's working for and against us, and on how we can better manage it. This doesn't have to be an extended period—ten or fifteen minutes of careful reflection can benefit us greatly, especially if done early in the day. And of course it can be included in our daily devotional time, if we have such a commitment (and if not, this is a great way to get started!). But the important things to consider are—

The past day's successes and failures. How well did you manage your feelings during the past day? Did you worry about something unnecessarily too much? Did you lose your temper or cave in to some other emotional hijacking? Did you say yes to someone for the wrong reasons, when you should have said no? Why did these incidents occur? And what can you learn from them to be wiser emotionally in the future?

On the positive side, did you manage a challenging emotional situation well? Commend yourself then, and enjoy the memory! And consider what you can learn from the incident to help you successfully handle similar situations in the future.

Challenges this current day may pose. Do you anticipate any situations today that may be difficult for you emotionally? Pray for Christ's strength and guidance to face them well. Consider how a given situation may unnerve you, then prepare yourself mentally to face it. Do you expect a particular meeting scheduled at work to stir your anger, for instance? Be ready to count to ten and hold your peace, if needed; or to speak your mind calmly and considerately, if appropriate.

Pray for Christ's help also with unexpected challenges that will surely arise during the day. Remind yourself of the need to question impulsive feelings, and to be careful your decisions are guided as much by your mind as by your heart. Preparing in this way for the day's emotional challenges can greatly help you to manage them successfully.

Other difficult situations you're facing. If you're dealing with a loss or defeat, reflect on any benefits that may come from it, and remind yourself of the resilience God gives you to rebound. If you need to take a step soon that frightens you, reflect on the strength Christ will give you to do it, plus any other reasons for taking courage. Pray for God's help as you need it in these situations.

Your desires and God's will. Plan at least once a week—on a weekend morning, perhaps—to extend this daily time, in order to focus on your emotions' positive role and the guidance they may be giving you about God's will. Think about whether you have a strong and long-standing desire to do something new with your life. And if so, does it match up well with your gifts and talents? Would it clearly help others? Such a longing may be the most important prompting God gives you to take a new direction. Here, it's not the stray inspiration you feel on a given day, but the one that has persisted and stood the test of time. Pray for Christ's wisdom in weighing its implications, and for the courage to move forward with any step of faith that's recommended.

Counseling?

If you're suffering from an emotional struggle or disorder that is getting the best of you, in spite of your most earnest efforts to manage it, seek the best professional help you can find for it. Prolonged depression, bipolar tendencies, PTSD symptoms, a debilitating phobia, unremitting anxiety or panic attacks, serious difficulty managing anger, or addictive behavior, each indicates a chronic condition that recommends professional assistance. There's no more shame in seeking a professional's help for a mental health issue than in seeking a doctor's assistance for a physical problem. Indeed, these afflictions usually have their physical side, and healing comes from a combination of medical help and counseling. If a serious emotional disorder is ruining your life, seek the level of help you need for conquering it. The right counselor, psychologist or psychiatrist can do you a world of good. Support groups also abound for each of these disorders, and can provide unspeakable benefits.

The Normative Experience for Most of Us

The more normal emotional struggles we all experience, day-in and day-out, respond well to the cognitive steps I'm suggesting, and usually don't require professional assistance—apart perhaps from an occasional time of personal crisis. The goal of living wiser emotionally is highly achievable, if we commit ourselves to the daily and constant practice of being self-aware. As our emotional intelligence grows, we are by default happier, more productive, and considerably more effective for Christ. There are at least five reasons we're more successful in everything we do:

1. As we grow to understand our feelings better, our instincts improve; we more naturally recognize what things we're most deeply motivated to do with our life, and through this understanding gain a vital window into God's will.

2. By projection, we more naturally perceive others' feelings accurately and resonate with them—the quality known as empathy, which is at the heart of genuine compassion and being able to love others effectively for Christ

3. Managing our feelings better makes us more likeable and approachable; our social skills naturally improve, leading to a wide range of benefits for the goals we take on.

4. We're much less distracted by negative feelings and much more buoyed by positive ones; in short, we have much more positive energy for the work we do, and for extending Christ's love to others.

5. We're less susceptible to a rescue mentality, and more likely to assume responsibility for the right reasons.

There are, in short, abundant reasons to commit ourselves wholeheartedly to the goal of growing wiser emotionally. Becoming more self-aware is both a highly achievable goal and highly rewarding. I urge you to make growing wiser emotionally a lifestyle. These steps will help you get started, and will allow you to reinvent your life in some very positive ways!

But Wait, There's More . . .
Emotional intelligence not only involves understanding how our emotions affect us, and striving to manage their influences as constructively as possible. It also involves coming to understand certain underlying assumptions we have about life, and our potential in different areas, which profoundly affect how we feel and what we choose to do—then revising these beliefs as needed. I'm talking here about default assumptions we seldom question, but which can be sadly misguided. When they are, they can diminish our joy in living, and greatly restrict the choices we make.

We come here to a fascinating and hugely important area, which will be our focus in the next two chapters.

2

Reshaping Assumptions That Shape Our Life

ONCE I WAS SCHEDULED TO SPEAK at a weekend conference near Spartanburg, South Carolina. Expecting this retreat to be unusually challenging, I felt stressed and, with other responsibilities on my plate just then, uneasy about taking the time away.

I was anxious as well about the ten-hour drive this trip required. To ease the travel burden, I left on Thursday evening and drove to South Hill, Virginia, where I spent the night in a motel. My anxiety about the conference, however, and a noisy room, resulted in a poor night's sleep. I left South Hill on Friday morning fatigued, wondering how I would ever muster the energy for the remaining seven-hour drive, and then run at full steam for the strenuous weekend ahead. I struggled to stay awake that whole trip, and had to stop and nap at one point.

Through sheer effort of will I finally made it to the conference center, and was on stage speaking shortly after that. Between speaking and counseling, I ran myself ragged that weekend, sleeping minimally Friday and Saturday nights. The event went well, though, and when I pulled away about 2:00 Sunday afternoon I felt encouraged, and much relieved my responsibilities were over.

At this point, what did I do? Check in to the nearest hotel and sleep for two days?

Not exactly.

I drove back to Maryland—straight—arriving home around midnight.

No nap this time—just one breeze through a McDonald's drive-through, and a couple of gas stops. The extreme fatigue I'd suffered on my trip south never set in on the way home, and I felt energetic for much of that drive.

It might seem illogical that I enjoyed this sudden gust of energy, when I felt bone-tired on Friday, then by Sunday had even more reason to be exhausted. But, of course, you're chuckling, because you've had this experience many times: You've dragged through a difficult workweek, sleeping poorly from the stress, wondering how you'll ever make it to the end of the workday Friday. By midweek you can only imagine that after work Friday, you'll go straight to bed and sleep through till noon Saturday. But at 5:00 p.m. Friday, you feel strangely revived. By 5:30 you're off to the gym for a vigorous workout, then out to dinner with friends, and chatting till 1:00 a.m. You bound out of bed at 7:30 Saturday morning to begin a remodeling project you've been longing to tackle; then go hiking with the kids Saturday afternoon; then to a party Saturday evening, lasting into the small hours. Never during this time does your energy seriously lag, because the joy of what you're doing carries you along.

We go through these episodes of fatigue and sudden rejuvenation often. Most of us are quite aware that we're capable of catching a "second wind," and we may be amazed and amused at just how dramatically our strength can revive for what we really want to do. Seldom, though, do we think clearly about this process, and consider its broader implications for our life.

When we do examine it carefully, we invariably find that our energy, both physically and emotionally, is profoundly affected by our expectations—day-in and day-out. On that Friday driving south, for instance, I simply assumed that a lousy night's sleep meant sure fatigue during a long drive to an event I regretted scheduling. With hindsight, it's obvious this assumption had more to do with the tiredness I felt than the loss of sleep itself—for otherwise the rush of energy I experienced on Sunday makes no sense. And that burst of steam also sprang from an expectation—the belief that I could draw on reserve energy for a ten-hour drive home and do just fine. In both instances, assumptions about my capabilities strongly influenced how energetic I felt.

Yet these were *default* assumptions in both cases, not outlooks I had carefully thought through and consciously chosen to embrace. In the same way, most of us go through life scarcely realizing how greatly certain underlying suppositions, largely unconscious, are affecting our vitality.

Premature Cognitive Commitments

Psychologists term these default expectations "premature cognitive commitments." In her inspiring book, *Mindfulness*,

Harvard psychologist Ellen J. Langer talks in detail about these preset mental attitudes and how they affect not only our energy, but our health, well-being and destiny in dramatic ways.[1] Each of us, Langer points out, carries certain deeply embedded convictions about our possibilities in life. We don't view them as "convictions," however—as beliefs we have purposely chosen to hold—but as *truths* about our existence, as obvious as the sun's dependable rising in the morning. Rarely do we question them or examine them or consider how they might be influencing us.

Yet influence us they do. Our health, energy, happiness, accomplishments, and success with people are far more affected by premature cognitive commitments than by our native abilities in these areas.

In some cases the effect is positive. Former president Ronald Reagan simply assumed that everyone he encountered would like him; this belief was part of the fabric of his personality. The results were intriguing, in that even his enemies were attracted to him socially. His arch-nemesis in Congress, Democratic leader Thomas "Tip" O'Neill, commented that while he hated Reagan's policies, on the personal level, "I find it impossible to dislike the guy."

At the other extreme, premature cognitive commitments too often work against us. A childhood friend, whom I considered brilliant when we were kids, in his mid-forties confessed to me that he had lived beneath his potential for much of his life. In sixth grade, he explained, his teacher belittled his work in such a way that left him convinced he was incapable of academic learning. That conviction, which he carried throughout his teenage years and into adulthood, caused him to avoid challenging courses in junior high and high school, to stay away from college, and to settle for a job that didn't tap his capabilities well. Only now was he beginning to revisit that assumption, and to realize just how greatly it had restricted his choices.

When we look carefully at our own life—at those areas where things go well for us, and at those where they don't—we so often find that certain expectations are affecting our behavior and its outcomes far more than we've realized. It helps us greatly to gain a better understanding of these assumptions, especially of those that hinder us unfairly. The good news is that we can change these expectations into ones that reflect the potential God truly has given us, and his bigger picture for our life. The results that we enjoy from such "paradigm shifts" can be astonishing, and life-changing in the most genuine sense.

Becoming fully aware of our default assumptions can take work, reflection and determination, and the help of a counselor or trusted friend can be invaluable in the process. Yet the task is typically not Herculean either. If our negative expectations spring from traumatic past experience, to be sure, the task of uncovering repressed memories may be painful, and may require special help. This is the extreme case, though.

Most often, our premature cognitive commitments—even our most negative ones—result simply from faulty thinking. They are perspectives we've adapted—for whatever reasons— because they made sense at one time, and we've held on to them mindlessly ever since. Pinpointing them doesn't require extended psychotherapy, nor is it necessary to understand when or why we latched on to them. All we need to understand is how our thinking is off the mark, and how it is hurting our life.

Far from being a painful undertaking, it's usually gratifying to discover these points where we've been shooting ourselves in the foot. We're more than happy to let go of assumptions that are defeating us, once we understand where our thinking is skewed.

Identifying our premature cognitive commitments is half the battle; the other half is reshaping our unduly pessimistic expectations into positive ones. We need to become strongly convinced that certain options are feasible for us, to the point that these convictions are inherent in our thinking. Let's look at how we can meet this challenge in several areas where premature cognitive commitments most obviously affect us.

Fatigue and Burnout

As suggested by my experience driving south, and many you've undoubtedly had, we often don't understand our capacity for energy well. We may be convinced that we have to feel tired, even horribly fatigued, given certain circumstances. Yet the exhaustion we feel on such occasions may have more to do with our expectations than our physical state.

We may fear we don't have the strength to carry out an unpleasant but necessary responsibility. Yet we should look carefully at our expectations. How do we *know* this task will tax us beyond our limits? Have there been times when we've found surprising vitality for something equally challenging that we *wanted* to do? If so, then we have that same capacity for energy now. Reminding ourselves that this is true may not bring a sudden, dramatic change in how we feel. Yet this insight can give us an extra edge and the courage to persevere, since we realize we're not likely to collapse or fall apart if we do. And with time and practice, by making a habit of thinking through challenges in this way, we can see our general vitality increase—as our expectations come more into line with our actual potential for energy.

A related issue has to do with "burnout." It has become popular in recent years (may I say, fashionable?) to speak of being burned out when we're highly stressed. The graphic imagery brought to mind by the term—a light bulb's filament's suddenly popping, or an engine's grinding to a halt from lack of oil—implies a dire condition: something has snapped within us; we're completely overextended, incapable of continuing, and in need of substantial rest to regain our strength.

There's no question we can reach a point of frustration or exhaustion in a role where our effectiveness is seriously hindered, and we need a break. But are we truly *burned out*? We're usually far more capable of resilience than the term suggests.

The assumption that we're capable of burning out is a powerful premature cognitive commitment that can leave us susceptible to thinking we're depleted beyond hope, when we may simply be tired and need a good night's sleep. This belief may also lead us to overreact in unfortunate ways; we may abandon an activity or goal that benefits us, when it would be to our advantage to stick with it.

A look at our past experience can show just how illusory this belief often is. Who among us who attended college, for instance, didn't reach a point toward the end of a semester when we felt so exhausted by our course work that we just wanted to quit? We wondered how we could possibly marshal the strength to complete our final projects and take our exams. Who, though, regrets pushing themselves a little harder to get through this period? And did we collapse once the semester was over? Of course not—we felt ready to take on the world!

Of course, part of what gets us through the difficult final stretch of a college semester is knowing that the burden isn't endless, and that we'll enjoy a break before long. When we're feeling highly stressed in other situations, the solution may be to give ourselves a respite, or to plan one to look forward to soon. The belief that we're burned out, though, may lead us to think that we need a major break, when in fact a brief one may serve us just as well.

Consider Elijah's experience in 1 Kings 19:1-8. Following one eventful day that included a horrific showdown with the prophets of Baal, intense praying for rain, and a twenty-mile jog to Ahab's palace, Elijah is understandably depleted beyond normal human limits. A veiled threat on his life from Queen Jezebel plunges the normally faith-buoyed prophet into suicidal depression. He leaves his servant behind and wanders a day's journey into the desert, where he collapses under the shade of a broom tree, asking God to take his life. He then falls asleep. After some time, perhaps a night's rest, an angel awakens him with food. Elijah eats, falls asleep again, then awakens once more to a fresh meal, again prepared by the angel. After just two or three days of solitude, sleep and good nourishment, Elijah finds his strength restored. "And he arose . . . and went in the strength of that food forty days and forty nights to Horeb the mount of God" (v. 8 RSV).

Elijah begins this episode convinced that he is stressed beyond all hope and healing. Yet it takes only a short retreat to revive his strength. His experience is good to keep in mind when we think we're at the end of our tether. We may indeed need some rest and refreshment. But a few days of quiet by the lake may benefit us as greatly as a three-month cruise.

If you're carrying the belief that life's challenges can easily burn you out, that expectation is certain to defeat you. Work at revising that conviction. Assume instead that you're capable of tiring, but not immeasurably so. Remind yourself that Christ has made you resilient, and that it's his nature to renew your strength and give you fresh heart for what he wants you to do. Focusing on these positive factors will help you to keep times of stress and fatigue in better perspective.

Issues of Health and Aging

Just as our expectations affect our energy, they influence our health in many ways. Most of us are generally aware that this is true; we recognize that a "placebo effect" occurs in medicine, for instance. Yet we tend to think of it as something other people experience. It can be surprising to discover just how susceptible to it we are personally.

In order to avoid stomach upset, I've developed the habit of chewing an antacid tablet before taking Advil for a headache. Then I chew a piece of gum to get rid of the antacid's taste. At least twice this past year I performed this initial ritual, then absentmindedly forgot to take the Advil—yet my headache still went away. My body responded positively to action it associated with vanquishing the pain, even though I never took the pain medicine itself. (If you've ever swallowed a painkiller in caplet form, then felt relief within minutes, you've had this identical experience, for it takes the pill about thirty minutes to metabolize!)

The discovery that we have a particular illness or physical problem brings with it the knowledge that certain symptoms may follow. We may experience them for reasons that are purely health-related. Yet our expectations can—and typically do—influence our perception of symptoms, and may lead us to place limitations on ourselves unnecessarily.

Legendary golfer Babe Didrikson Zaharias contracted cancer at age 42, then underwent a colostomy. Six weeks following her surgery she won the Beaumont Open of 1953, then won five more pro tour events the following year. Never mind that the cancer had spread throughout her body during this time; her doctor hadn't informed her that the disease had fully metastasized, nor that she was supposed to be dead by the time she won the competitions in 1954.

Hers is a fascinating example of how the *true* restraints of an illness or physical problem vary greatly from person to person, and of how one's experience can defy conventional wisdom. The lesson for each of us is to be cautious in how we think about our limitations. We should be slow to conclude that any limitation we imagine we have is genuine, apart from convincing proof.

The power of suggestion has such a radical effect on our health and physical well-being that we need to take special care to embrace positive expectations in this area. Several steps can help:

• *Focus on God as a healer.* Scripture never guarantees that God will heal every infirmity we experience. God denied Paul's request to remove the thorn in his side, and refused to grant David's plea to spare the life of the son that Bathsheba bore to him. Still, we find an overwhelming emphasis on God's healing in Scripture—as though biblical writers are saying that healing is the norm, not the exception, when we ask for it. This focus on healing comes across in many ways. Most prayers for healing in the Bible were granted; Jesus never denied a single request for healing during his earthly ministry, and spent more time healing physical and emotional problems than he did teaching; Paul himself performed impressive healing miracles; Psalm 103 declares that God heals all our diseases and renews our youth "like the eagle's" (v. 5); and James notes that the prayer of faith will heal the sick person (Jas 5:15).

In both its examples and teaching, Scripture gives far more attention to God's healing than to the case when he refrains from healing for a special purpose. What this pattern suggests is that we should feel tremendous freedom to pray continually and hopefully for God's healing of the physical problems we experience. We should put the burden of proof on God to show us if his intent is not to heal us, and that we should simply accept a physical problem as his will. Thus, Paul felt great liberty to continue praying earnestly for God to remove the thorn from his side until God clearly told him it must remain (2 Cor 12:7-10).

An inclination toward expecting God's healing and physical empowering will contribute significantly to our health and vitality, and will enhance the freedom we feel to seek his help.

• *Choose optimistic doctors.* Few exercise the power of suggestion more powerfully in our lives than doctors and other medical professionals. Who among us hasn't at some time feared we were experiencing the symptoms of a certain illness, only to find them disappear soon after a physician told us they were of no concern?

If we're less fortunate, we've felt like we were handed a death sentence when a doctor with poor communication skills informed us that we had a serious condition. Such was the case with a close friend of mine, who a year ago was told in ominous tones by a urologist that he had advanced prostate cancer, two years to live, and no meaningful alternatives for treatment. For about a month he lived with this conclusion, deeply depressed. Then he decided to seek further evaluation. Other specialists saw his condition more hopefully, and insisted there was plenty he could do to fight it. He pursued the most aggressive treatment available. Today he is free of all symptoms, and doctors working with him are offering a much more optimistic prognosis than he was initially given.

We may not be able to change how suggestible we are around medical personnel. But we can choose which ones we consult with, and thus the "suggestions" to which we're exposed. To the fullest extent possible, we should employ doctors and specialists who not only are clearly competent but optimistic in how they view our condition, and who have a knack for inspiring us to stay hopeful. And we should never accept any doctor's gloomy forecast without seeking further opinions.

• *Stay optimistic about aging.* It's just as important to choose doctors, friends and associates who are optimistic about our possibilities in later years. Countless studies have shown that elderly people who continue to assume responsibility for their needs, have interesting work to do, and believe they are needed, are better off. They enjoy better health and vitality, and live longer, than those who don't enjoy these advantages. Many studies have shown, too, that long-held notions about certain areas of potential having to decline in later age are simply erroneous, or grossly exaggerated. Our expectations greatly affect how productive we remain into our senior years, and thus how meaningful life continues to be for us.

I recall an elderly neighbor who had to relinquish her driver's license due to cataracts. She had no immediate family living to care for her—a fact that often discouraged her. Yet she also had no one telling her she was too old to be doing certain things and must let others do them for her. Instead, she had a large number of younger friends in her ethnic community who looked up to her as a matriarchal figure with great respect. So about two years later she had cataract surgery, took her driver's test, passed and became a road warrior again. Edwina was 95.

Examples like hers are immensely inspiring, for they encourage us not to sell our possibilities short as we age. They remind us too of the importance of having those around us who continue to believe in us as life moves on.

Success and Failure

Of course, we need this sort of positive reinforcement throughout our lives, and in all of our important pursuits. Our success or failure at every point where we seek to follow a dream, accomplish a goal or be productive, is to a large extent a product of our expectations.

Some of us are natural optimists. Just as Ronald Reagan expected others to like him, we assume we'll inevitably succeed in certain endeavors, and our expectations enhance the positive results we often experience.

But most of us have to work at being optimistic. Like my friend who from sixth grade on assumed that he couldn't be educated, we may be carrying expectations throughout our life that are deeply hindering our potential. How can we identify and relinquish these hurtful convictions? The best step we can take is to focus, not on uncovering our blind spots *per se*, but on better understanding the potential God truly has given us. He has endowed us each with certain natural abilities. He also inspires each of us uniquely—to enjoy certain work, and to accomplish certain objectives with our life. As our insight grows into how God has gifted and motivated us, we'll invariably discover those points where negative assumptions have been defeating us.

We should seek the best help available in this process of discovering our potential. We live in a fortunate era, when well-conceived vocational tests can help us fine-tune our understanding—both of our native ability and of the motivational tendencies that are most central to our personality. Competent vocational counseling is also widely available. We ought to avail ourselves of such resources to the fullest extent we need them.

As we come to better understand our potential, we should set goals that reflect the gifts and interests that God most clearly has given us. It's important also to "rehearse" these goals often—to review them in our devotional time, and to bring them to mind frequently throughout the day. We should remind ourselves why, given how God has fashioned us, these goals make sense for us, and why we have strong reason to be optimistic about accomplishing them.

In the ongoing process of embracing our goals and fine-tuning them, we should also seek to spend as much time as possible with friends and acquaintances who think encouragingly about us. Their expectations invariably influence our own, and God will often use them to help clarify his will for us.

Finally—and it's hard to stress this point too strongly—we should give special priority to spending regular time alone with

Christ, in which we allow him ample opportunity to clarify his will and to give us fresh heart for what he wants us to do. The conviction that Christ wants us to take a certain step with our life is the most positive, powerful expectation we can embrace. This confidence can come as we seek his presence and make a responsible effort to establish goals that reflect his best for us. It's all part of exercising stewardship over the life he has entrusted to us.

Summary

Each of us carries certain assumptions about life and our own potential—premature cognitive commitments—that profoundly affect our well-being, success and destiny, but which typically are largely unconscious and unexamined. Too often they work against us. And where life seems to be chronically working against us, these underlying expectations are often at fault. But the wonderful news is that with the right effort, we can reshape them into ones that are more life-giving, and which contribute more greatly to our happiness and productivity. And so making the effort to understand them and revise them where needed makes enormous sense.

In the next chapter we'll look at another stunning example of a premature cognitive commitment that can either shut down our initiative or stimulate it—our assumption about unwelcome events and what they signify. This will further demonstrate the powerful effect our underlying assumptions have upon our destiny for good or ill.

3

Embracing Optimism

YOU'RE DRIVING TO WORK and pull into the company lot. There at the entrance your car grinds to a stop and won't restart. You call for a tow truck, which hauls your lame vehicle to a repair shop across town. An hour later they phone with the diagnosis: a blown head gasket—a $2,000 repair. So much for that ski vacation you've been planning.

You're not five minutes into mulling your misfortune when the phone rings again. Now it's the school nurse; your ten-year-old is feeling nauseous and needs to see a doctor.

Your supervisor, already annoyed at how much time you've spent fussing with your car, scowls when you ask for leave to deal with Kerry's emergency.

You hail a cab, which takes a circuitous route to the repair shop. There, you're told that the loaner car you were promised is in use and won't be back for a while. You're left to sit and stew for an hour and worry that your daughter may have meningitis.

When you finally reach the school, Kerry informs you she feels fine now and doesn't want to leave. Besides, it's lunchtime and they're serving sausage pizza.

"Don't even ask," you announce as you make your office reentry at 1:30 p.m. Only to find that an important file you'd forgotten to save in rushing to leave is no longer on your hard drive—lost in the great digital divide.

You feel obliged to work late to finish your assignments. When you finally arrive home at 8:30 p.m., a strange odor greets you and draws you immediately to the basement. You find the source all too quickly: muck in the shower stall. Your septic tank has backed up.

You trudge back upstairs and collapse in a living room chair. Can anything else possibly go wrong? Of course it can. Muffy. Where's Muffy?

A moment later Kerry runs in to announce she'd forgotten to close the kitchen door, and your English Spaniel has escaped. Soon a neighbor phones with follow-up news: Muffy has been crafting craters in her beautifully landscaped front yard.

So it goes with certain days. We've all been through them. Those horrid occasions when everything hits the fan.

Sometimes it doesn't all happen in a single day, but in close enough succession that we feel our life is uniquely cursed. In the past two weeks Rita has (a) lost her job through company downsizing; (b) suffered the breakup of a two-year relationship she'd hoped would end in marriage; (c) learned that a graduate program she wanted to enter doesn't have room for her; (d) watched a stock on which she had pinned her investment hopes decline 65 percent.

Of course, it may not take events as dramatic as these nor as many to make us fear our life is in a downward spiral. We're fragile as humans. Two or three misfortunes in a row may leave us wondering.

There are two ways we may interpret the bad days or bad periods we inevitably experience. We may conclude it's simply too coincidental that several calamities have struck us in a row. There's obviously a message in this unfortunate sequence: the bottom is falling out of our life; God is against us; we better brace ourselves for further hard times ahead.

Or we may view these events as aberrations. They're exceptions to our normal experience—out-of-the-ordinary setbacks that, by the law of averages, occasionally occur in close succession in anyone's life. There's no direct connection between them, and no message about God's will or our destiny implied. The only message is that we have some work to do to solve some problems. These hardships won't have a long-term negative effect on our life unless we allow them to.

A Message in Adverse Circumstances?

These two views reflect two outlooks in psychology. Some with a Jungian background see events in our lives that otherwise seem unrelated as linked in a mystical way. *Synchronicity* is the positive side of it. A series of welcome events, however unconnected they might appear, are life's means of helping us succeed. They indicate we're enjoying a fortuitous period, and that the timing is good for us to press toward cherished goals.

Asynchrony is the other extreme, when everything is falling apart. One psychologist explains: "Asynchrony is the opposite of synchronicity. We become aware, through a series of negating coincidences, that this is the wrong time for ventures. Nothing works; doors keep closing. We find ourselves involved in wars of attrition, obeying laws of diminishing returns. . . . Reading the handwriting on the wall is often a way of describing asynchrony, an indication that this is not the time for success but rather that our time is almost up in this area and we are ready for new options elsewhere."[1]

Many Jungians would say that a sequence of events such as the bad day we've just imagined, or Rita's bad period, indicates that life is not working well for us at this time. It's giving us a message to slow down and hibernate a bit. We shouldn't press an important cause right now, but should wait for more auspicious indications. Life may be revealing where we need to grow and modify our behavior, too, even if we did nothing directly to cause our misfortunes. Going with the flow of life is critical, and reflecting on the lessons in the fallout is essential.

A strong challenge to such fatalistic thinking comes from another field of psychology. Martin Seligman, and the positive psychology movement he has founded, stress the importance of not reading undo significance into negative events. When bad things happen to us, Seligman explains, we instinctively reason outwardly from them in inappropriate ways. We assume the pattern is "pervasive" (things are going badly in all areas of my life), that it will be "perpetual" (continuing indefinitely), and that the reason for it is "personal" (we blame ourselves for problems we did nothing to bring about).[2]

If we're to attain the optimism that leads to mental health and success, Seligman insists, we must break with our tendency to draw unwarranted conclusions from life's unhappy events. If we're obviously at fault for what has happened, we should learn what we can from our mistake and move on. We must be careful not to browbeat ourselves unreasonably or to blame ourselves when there's no reason for doing so. Especially important, we shouldn't infer connections between unwelcome events that aren't plainly there nor expect that the pattern is fated to repeat. We ought to view such events as exceptions; if we regard them as the norm, our belief will become a self-fulfilling prophecy. We have considerable control over our destiny, if we'll not allow setbacks to discourage us from moving toward our goals.

Being alert to these differences in philosophy is important if we seek counseling, for different counselors, given the same information, may advise us in different ways, depending on their orientation.

Understanding these two points of view also helps us to clarify our own perspective on personal misfortune. Most of us respond to life's unwelcome events in an instinctive fashion we don't fully understand. We may despair after suffering a setback or two, yet not recognize why we're so susceptible to discouragement. The underlying problem may be a philosophy of life more akin to Jungian thinking than Seligman's. Appreciating how we're thinking underneath is invaluable, for it gives us the freedom to examine our outlook and, if it's working against us, to modify it.

Faith and Optimism

Where we come out on the matter as a Christian strongly affects our outlook of faith, and whether we believe God is allowing us control to remedy problems in our life and to accomplish our goals and dreams. We tend as believers to tilt more toward a Jungian perspective. This inclination springs in part from our understanding of God's providence—that nothing happens in our life outside of his control. That belief leads us to read meaning into events that affect us and to try to interpret them. When we experience several disappointments in a row, it's natural to conclude that God has a message for us in the pattern.

The message may be that he doesn't want us to succeed, and that we should stop kicking against the goad by trying. Or, worse, we may conclude that God is punishing us for our misdeeds. That conviction is often fed by Scriptural teaching that we're too quick to apply personally. The early chapters of the Old Testament are filled with warnings that God will repay serious disobedience by bringing wholesale calamity upon one's life (Deut 28:15-68).

These warnings can pose a particular challenge for Christians who are at all sensitive or analytical by nature. We typically become more conscious of our sin and vulnerability as we grow in Christ—a consequence of coming closer to his light and being exposed by it. The result is that we can be more inclined to think, as a more mature Christian, that the impending-doom Bible passages might apply to us, than we might imagine as a younger believer. It doesn't take much in the way of misfortune to make us worry that the dam has finally broken: we've pushed God's patience beyond the limit, and now he's paying us back. And if that's true, then the fallout is likely to continue—so we better knuckle under and accept it.

This was not the mentality of Christians in the New Testament. It was emphatically not the way Paul viewed hardships in his own life. He did experience them. In 2 Corinthians 11 he rehearses some examples:

> Five times I have received at the hands of the Jews the forty lashes less one. Three times I have been beaten with rods; once I was stoned. Three times I have been shipwrecked; a night and a day I have been adrift at sea; on frequent journeys, in danger from rivers, danger from robbers, danger from my own people, danger from Gentiles, danger in the city, danger in the wilderness, danger at sea, danger from false brethren; in toil and hardship, through many a sleepless night, in hunger and thirst, often without food, in cold and exposure. And apart from other things, there is the daily pressure upon me of my anxiety for all the churches. (vv 24-28 RSV)

It is striking that Paul, in reflecting on these and other calamities he suffered, never suggests that God brought any about in order to punish him. Paul would have had a profound basis for this conclusion. He was an intensely analytical Christian, acutely aware of his own continuing sin, as he graphically explains in Romans 7. If he didn't regard his troubles as God's judgment for sins of the present, he could easily have seen them as punishment for sins of the past. Yet Paul never leaned toward such an outlook.

Nor did he ever view setbacks as God's effort to thwart his long-term aspirations. If one opportunity to evangelize failed to materialize, he simply looked for a new one and kept knocking on doors till one opened (Acts 16:6-10).

When Paul did reflect on God's purpose behind his trials, he always reached optimistic conclusions. His hardships were God's way of building empathy in him (2 Cor 1:3-7); the thorn in his side was God's means of helping him rely more fully on

his grace (2 Cor 12:7-10); his imprisonment was an opportunity to share about Christ with the palace guard and to strengthen
the courage of other Christians through his example (Phil 1:12-
14). In most cases, though, it seems that Paul didn't get finely
analytical about his hardships, but he saw them as going with
the territory in the life God had ordained him to live. And he
wasn't thrown off course when they occurred one after another
in rapid fire, but was inclined to fight all the harder.

Perhaps most important, when Paul experienced setbacks,
he didn't draw connections between them that weren't apparent, nor jump to the conclusion that fallout was inevitable
throughout his life. He remained remarkably optimistic that God
would remedy his problems and open new doors where others
had closed.

Reasons for Resilience

Paul's example, then, is extraordinarily encouraging to consider
at times when unwelcome circumstances broadside our life. It
suggests that, if Christ is our Lord, we're not obliged to fatalistic thinking about them. Paul would say, I'm certain, that the
effort to connect the dots between them that some encourage is
inappropriate for the Christian whose heart's intent is to follow
Christ. It discourages positive action, and is more akin to superstition than to biblical faith. Seligman has it right in saying we
shouldn't invent connections between events that aren't unde-
niably there.

I believe Paul would say to those of us who suffer a truly
bad day, or a series of disappointments such as Rita did, that
successive hardships are occasionally our lot as humans. But
they don't force us to any gloomy conclusion about God's hand

in our life. In fact, by the law of averages, and by the always surprising providence of God, we may just as well be in line for a breakthrough now as anything.

In addition to his robust example, Paul notes principles in his writings that help to clarify his outlook toward setbacks, and that provide us a further basis for viewing our own optimistically.

• *"He who began a good work in you will carry it on to completion until the day of Christ Jesus" (Phil 1:6).* Overriding all of Paul's exhortations to believers is a supreme conviction that God takes extreme initiative to hold on to those whom he chooses to belong to Christ, and to nurture and mature them. For me to imagine that, as a follower of Christ, I've sinned so badly that the Old Testament's impending-doom passages apply to me, is to suggest that God is exercising less power to keep me on track than he has promised he would.

There's an irony to consider, too. If I had fallen to the point that God was bringing wholesale fallout to my life, I'd not likely be concerned about my relationship with him at all. The fact that I'm worried I may have pushed his patience beyond the limit suggests it hasn't happened.

• *"God is not the author of confusion" (1 Cor 14:33 KJV).* Paul was the last one to claim that God never disciplines Christians for their disobedience. But Paul also understood God as being concerned that believers come to the clearest possible knowledge of his truth. This suggests his chastisement will not be so vague that we're likely to misinterpret it.

It's fair to assume that if God wants to teach me a lesson about certain misbehavior, the lesson will be plain. If he wishes to discipline me through bringing about certain consequences, these will be obviously related to what I've done wrong—so that I'm not left guessing about his intentions.

If I become intoxicated, then drive recklessly and wreck my car, the consequences in this case result directly from my behavior. It's reasonable to assume they are God's chastisement. But to think that my car engine's overheating this afternoon is God's punishment for lustful thoughts I indulged this morning is stretching things and a superstitious conclusion, since there's no obvious way my fantasies caused this mechanical problem. I should assume that if God wants to discipline me for my thought life, he'll not use an event so purely random.

• *"In all things God works for the good of those who love him, who have been called according to his purpose" (Rom 8:28)*. Paul speaks more exuberantly here than anywhere else about God's providential role in the Christian's life. While he indicates that nothing escapes God's notice, he stresses that God has infinitely positive intentions in all the events that touch our experience. Paul never suggests that this is a reason to repress our discouragement or to engage in insincere praise talk that betrays our feelings; he spoke at different times of feeling great frustration personally, and on one occasion of despairing of life itself (2 Cor 1:8).

Still, the principle strongly steers us away from ominous speculation, when we suffer disappointment, about God's having turned against us. We're encouraged to take a deep breath, to look for the silver linings, and to keep a jury-is-out mentality about setbacks that presently seem to have no redeeming value. The principle is liberating, for it frees us from any obligation to draw disheartening connections between unrelated hardships.

• *"For by grace you have been saved through faith" (Eph*

2:8 RSV). Paul speaks extensively throughout his writings of the importance of faith. While we are saved by grace, it is grace received *through faith*. There are no benefits provided by Christ that we are not expected to attain by faith. This faith, as Paul and Scripture understand it, is an attitude that expects the best of God, and believes he has the most positive intentions conceivable for our life. It is demonstrated profoundly by individuals in the Gospels whom Jesus commended for their faith, who believed against the strongest odds that he would heal them and lift them out of the ruts into which they had fallen.

The most difficult problem with the notion of asynchrony is that it diminishes faith. There is a certain faith in the belief that negative events are giving us a message about our destiny, true. Yet it falls short of the vigorous faith of Scripture, which sees beyond immediate circumstances to God's bigger picture. It focuses too greatly on these circumstances—making them idols, conveyers of guidance—when in fact we see only the faintest tip of the iceberg in terms of all God is doing related to our life.

Martin Seligman's outlook, by discouraging our making connections between unrelated setbacks, doesn't guarantee faith will develop. Yet it clears the way for it, by removing a habit of thinking that stands in the way. We may take heart in knowing that faith mandates us to fight against handwriting-on-the-wall type thinking, and to strive for positive expectations about our future.

Riding Out the Storm

I had an unforgettable day some years ago when everything went wrong. The Sons of Thunder were scheduled to present a concert that evening in Columbia, Maryland. One of our key singers had laryngitis. Our keyboard player was delayed by an emergency at work and unable to make setup or practice; we bit our fingernails all afternoon wondering if he would arrive in time for the concert. The sound system gave us major problems that we couldn't resolve.

These were the small headaches. The big one: It was March 14, 1999, and the Washington region was in the grip of its first major late-winter snowstorm in decades. Driving was treacherous, and most churches were canceling their evening programs. We had scheduled the concert for mid-March precisely to avoid such weather, which rarely occurs here this late in the season. So we had an easy out. No one would have criticized us if we'd called off the concert, and we could have concluded God was prompting us to do so. We decided to go ahead with it, though, with a grim sense that the show must go on.

There was a magic present that evening that is difficult to describe, but was apparent to all who attended. Our keyboardist showed up at the last minute, in time to perform. The singer with laryngitis found unexpected strength once on stage, and the audience rallied behind her. The technical problems with the sound system abated during the concert and didn't hinder us.

About one hundred people showed up—a small attendance for the auditorium but a gratifying one considering the weather. The blanket of snow outside lent an intimacy to the evening and a survivor spirit to those who had braved the storm. The result was an energized, appreciative audience, to whom the band responded, playing with great heart.

When the concert was over, we were exceedingly glad we'd proceeded with it and hadn't let the ominous circumstances deter us. That evening will remain forever on the short list of my most cherished Sons of Thunder memories.

That experience, similar to many I've had performing music, reflects what ours is in life so often. We think the bottom is about to fall out of our life, but we press on to find success just around the corner.

I'm not suggesting there aren't times when the force of circumstances should compel us to slow down, to change direction or let go of a goal. Yet it should truly be the *force* of circumstances that prompts us to do so, not a spiritualized conclusion about them.

When in doubt, we should err on the side of continuing to pursue a goal or dream. Our potential to fall into despair is so substantial, that it's a good rule of thumb to assume things aren't as bleak as we're projecting. This point is especially important to keep in mind when bad days or difficult periods set in, for these are the times when circumstances are most likely to color our perception unfairly. We should remind ourselves constantly that God sees our life in infinitely more positive fashion than we do. And because we never know what he has around the next corner until we turn it, we do well to keep our life in motion and not let disappointment shut us down.

Bad days and hard experiences—what do they mean?

It's much more up to us to decide than we realize.

What we decide affects our destiny far more greatly than we imagine.

Our constant challenge is to see beyond our immediate situation and to view our life with the eyes of faith. Much of the battle is won simply by avoiding pessimistic thinking. We should make it a habit to question the connections we naturally draw between frustrating events, and to let go of any that aren't clearly justified.

Even more important, we should take whatever steps will best enable us to focus on Christ and to gain his outlook on our life. Spending time quietly in his presence, more than anything, helps us to gain a faith-centered perspective.

The next time you feel that your life is falling apart, devote some generous time to being still before him. Give him the fullest possible opportunity to influence your thinking.

That's making the right connection.

Conclusion

The way we interpret unwelcome events in our life—especially a succession of them—is a fascinating example of a premature cognitive commitment, and one that profoundly affects our happiness and sense of personal control. At one extreme, we assume these events are related, that we're fated to suffer them, and that they carry a message about more hard times to come. At the other extreme, we regard them as unrelated, not conveying a message about our future, and not stifling our initiative to improve our life in any way. It's a dramatic example of how our default assumptions work, and why it's vital to strive to understand and revise the ones that are working against us.

I hope our discussion so far has inspired you to examine the broad assumptions you carry about your life and your possibilities, and to carefully consider whether they reflect reality and respect the potential God has actually given you. This sort of self-scrutiny is a key part of growing wiser emotionally and reaping the considerable benefits emotional intelligence brings.

II

Emotional Intelligence:
Ten Liberating
Perspectives

4

Thinking Sanely About Our Emotional Life

MALCOLM HATED HIS JOB as much as anyone I've known. Though many would find house painting enjoyable, to him it was just a means of paying the rent. He sat slumped in the chair across from my desk, bemoaning his lot.

Yet Malcolm was a Christian who wanted God's will. So I stopped him and asked, "If God rolled out the red carpet and said you could be in any career you wished, which would it be?"

He didn't have to think long. He shot back, "I'd like to be an English teacher."

Malcolm had two years of college behind him. I was confident he could go back, finish and find a job in the public school system. So I said, "You're young enough to do it. Why don't you pursue teaching with all the passion and energy you can muster?"

His reply was unforgettable. "I know that God doesn't want

me teaching. I'd enjoy the experience too much. And the affirmation of students would be more than I could handle." Then he added the clincher: He was certain God wanted him painting houses, for he thoroughly disliked his work!

Growing wise emotionally means learning to manage our emotions well (chapter one), and it involves, when needed, revising certain underlying assumptions that broadly affect our well-being and potential (chapters two and three). It also means learning to think soundly in a wide number of other areas that affect our emotional life and mental health. We need, for one thing, sane perspectives on our different emotions themselves: What do they signify—about our life, about God's intentions for us, about potential action we should take? How can they mislead us, and where are we vulnerable? These outlooks need to be both biblically sound and reflective of how God has designed human life.

We see in my friend Malcolm—in a story from my *Faith and Optimism*—a classic example of distorted thinking about an emotion, in his case with tragic consequences. He assumed all human desire is sinful. By default, then, God wanted him to follow a career he disliked, and to avoid any he loved. Yet he overlooked a vital aspect of biblical teaching on desire. Of course our desires can beguile us, and the Bible is abundantly clear about that. But Scripture also stresses that a longstanding desire to *do something productive with our life* likely signals God's prompting, not his prohibition. Yet even respected Christian teachers sometimes miss this point. A major biblical seminar I once sat through, attended by hundreds of thousands nationwide, had as one of its guiding slogans: "God's will: the exact opposite of my natural inclinations."

Malcolm's example underscores our critical need to examine what we think about our different emotions, and to revise any misguided notions. We need to strive to understand what Scripture truly teaches about them, and what practical experience suggests as well.

In striving for emotional intelligence, we also need a good understanding of what steps will help tame our anxieties and boost our optimism and confidence. Does working on our self-talk help, for instance, and does it bring more than a cursory benefit?

In addition, we need a good grasp of how our emotional state influences our cognitive. How can we manage our life emotionally in a way that best enhances our ability to solve problems and recognize God's guidance? Here, the effect of our mood on our practical thinking is often stunning.

Once I faced a major challenge involving a conference my ministry was planning. Though I wrestled with how to solve this problem for weeks, there seemed to be no logical solution. Then our family went on vacation and spent a restful, refreshing week at the beach. On the morning of the last day, I woke up with a clear answer to my problem in mind. The solution—which in time proved ideal—was so obvious and simple that it was remarkable I hadn't thought of it before.

This is a good example of how our creative process so often works. God has given us minds capable of deriving good solutions and discerning his guidance. Yet our emotional state profoundly affects our ability to think constructively. Our mind may be quite ready to provide the perfect answer if we just allow it the opportunity—yet we can try too hard. Relaxing, changing our setting and giving it a little time, can bring surprising results. Learning to work with our natural problem-solving process helps us greatly in finding solutions and clarifying God's will.

Ten Liberating Perspectives

In this section I want to look at ten life-giving perspectives on our emotional life that can benefit us in countless ways. While we glanced at some of these briefly in chapter one, it will help now to examine them in greater detail. Eight concern several of our specific emotions, one the value of self-talk in managing our feelings, and one the impact of our emotional state on our ability to solve problems and recognize God's will. Each of these are areas where we can fall into unhealthy thinking that makes it difficult to manage our feelings well or to reap their benefits. It's hard to exaggerate the difference clear-headed outlooks can make at each of these points.

We'll devote a chapter to each of these perspectives, and they include—

1. The emotion of anger, while dangerous, is not sinful.

2. Ventilating anger more often nurtures it than relieves it; expressing anger complicates our life more often than not, and we should carefully weigh the likely results before doing so.

3. The greater our passion for a certain goal or dream, the greater our potential for acting in a self-defeating way, and the greater our need for others' assistance.

4. God guides us not only through the desires of our heart, but through our frustrations as well.

5. We each have a certain potential for despair, which we need to monitor and manage carefully; appreciating the deceptive nature of this emotion helps us break its spell.

6. God has gifted each of us with substantial resilience; our

potential to bounce back from a defeat—and even to benefit from it—is much greater than we typically realize.

7. Most of us invest vast energy into worrying about what others think; facing how misplaced most of this apprehension is brings relief, and allows us to take further steps to tame this "normal paranoia."

8. If you're prone to mood swings and mixed emotions, there's a positive side to this personality trait that's important to understand.

9. While working on our self-talk brings some benefit in managing our emotions, careful reflection on our life and our relationship with Christ brings much more.

10. God has created our minds to think constructively, to find good solutions and to recognize his guidance; yet we have to position ourselves emotionally for this to happen—and often the secret is simply to be in motion.

I should stress that these are just ten topics among a great many related to emotional intelligence that we could consider. Growing wise emotionally is a lifetime effort, and it would take many books to cover all the issues. I've chosen these specific concerns in part because they have been of interest to me in my own study, and in part because they are very common areas where we fall into misguided thinking, especially as Christians. There are also enough benefits to be gained from developing sane perspectives in these particular areas, to limit our focus to them in this book.

So let's look at these ten perspectives now, and at how they can open us more fully to Christ's abundant life.

(*Chapter 9 on despair is borrowed from my* Reach Beyond Your Grasp, *and chapter 13 on Self-Talk from* Faith and Optimism*)*.

5

Is Anger
A Sin?

IT HAPPENED AGAIN. Something I've heard so often. A friend told me another Christian had advised her that her angry feelings are sinful. Hearing that my friend had been counseled this way made me feel, well . . . angry.

Now that I've made this confession, I must hasten to say that I don't think I was sinning merely by *feeling* angry at that moment—although the potential for saying or doing something unkind was certainly there.

The assumption that the feeling of anger is sinful is so deeply embedded in Christian thinking that many never question it. It's the instinctive belief of many who haven't looked carefully at biblical teaching on anger. I don't deny that some are able to hold this belief without serious danger to their well-being. And it restrains some from acting out their anger in hurtful ways.

For many, the effect is far less fortunate. Not a few Christians go through life feeling guilty for each experience of angry feelings.

Take the case of Christine. Several in her office tease her about being a Christian. Two of her coworkers are particularly insensitive, and crack jokes that Christine finds offensive. Since Christine believes that a Christian shouldn't experience angry feelings—let alone express them—she bites her tongue and tries to act pleasant whenever her office mates make fun of her. Although she prays for charitable feelings toward them, she still feels resentful. Then she gets angry at herself for feeling bitter.

This vicious emotional cycle exhausts Christine and intensifies the anger she feels toward her associates. On several occasions, she has erupted angrily at them. These outbursts have deepened her self-disdain, and left her fellow employees even more skeptical about her faith.

Ironically, Christine's assumption that feeling angry is off limits for a Spirit-filled Christian is a major part of the problem. Her constant self-judgment makes it difficult for her to face her feelings honestly and control them. If Christine regarded anger as normal and acceptable, she would be able to own her feelings better, and to express them appropriately to her coworkers before she lost control.

Missing the Point

The belief that we sin by feeling angry is usually derived from Jesus' familiar statement in the Sermon on the Mount:

"You have heard that it was said to the men of old, 'You shall not kill; and whoever kills shall be liable to judgment.' But I say to you that every one who is angry with his brother shall be liable to judgment; whoever insults his brother shall be liable to the council, and whoever says, 'You fool!' shall be liable to the hell of fire." (Mt 5:21-22 RSV)

On the surface, Jesus does seem to say that the emotion of anger is sinful in itself—as condemnable as a murderous act that might spring from it. In the same spirit, he seems to indict the feeling of lust as tantamount to the sin of adultery, several verses later (Mt 5:27-28).

When we look beyond the Sermon on the Mount, however, we find other New Testament passages which show that negative emotions can occur without sin being present. Thus Paul declares, "Be angry but do not sin; do not let the sun go down on your anger" (Eph 4:26 RSV). Paul clearly indicates that we can feel angry without sinning. How can this be?

The usual Christian response is that we experience two types of anger: "righteous indignation" and "sinful anger." One is directed at a noble cause, the other at a selfish one; one is admirable, the other deplorable.

Scripture, though, never makes this distinction, which ignores the nature of human motivation. Pride and hurt feelings can run as deep in righteous indignation as in any other type of anger. Anger is the same emotion, whether evoked by a righteous concern or a dishonorable one. I frankly wish we would throw the term righteous indignation out of our Christian vocabulary; far too much self-righteousness is encouraged by it.

But how, then, does Paul's counsel to be angry but not sin reconcile with Jesus' teaching on anger in the Sermon on the Mount? Here it's important to note what Jesus says and what he doesn't. He doesn't say that the person who is angry is being judged as sinning, but that he is "liable to judgment." *Liable.*

He or she is at a highly vulnerable point—a hair's breadth, perhaps, from doing something rash. But this is different from saying that this person is *sinning* simply by feeling angry. This point is well-captured by Vernon Grounds in his *Emotional Problems and the Gospel:*

> Does our Lord mean that a mere feeling of anger is no different from the actual crime of murder? He can scarcely mean . . . that. No, He is reminding us, rather, of what can happen if an angry feeling is allowed to fester in our minds. . . . He is also counseling us to be on guard against the illusion that as His disciples, we no longer have those drives and impulses that can break out into violence.[1]

Jesus' point, then, isn't that anger is a sinful emotion but a *dangerous* one. When we examine the New Testament thoroughly on the point, in fact, we never find it condemning any emotion as sinful in itself. It's always the action which proceeds from an emotion that is judged sinful. Again, *"Be angry but do not sin."*

In this same spirit, James speaks of sin occurring when lust has "conceived" (Jas 1:15 KJV). And when Jesus declares in the Sermon on the Mount that a man who "looks" upon a woman lustfully commits adultery, he isn't referring to the mere feeling of sexual desire but to an *intentional* look. This is clear in the Greek, where the emphasis is upon the action of looking; sin occurs when I choose to nurture the feeling of lust, not merely through the emotion itself.

Accepting the Feeling

The point is more than an academic or semantic one. If we believe that the feeling of anger is sinful, we'll be inclined to judge ourselves unfairly whenever we feel angry. We'll assume God is displeased with us, and we may find it harder to approach him for help. We'll be likely to repress the feeling of anger, with all the psychological backlash that can result, and we'll be sitting ducks for the sort of emotional cycle Christine experiences.

If we can accept our feelings of anger as normal, human, and not condemned by God, then we'll find it easier to own these emotions, work through them and move beyond them. Here Scripture gives us not only a doctrinal basis for accepting our feelings but extensive examples as well. Many of the most impressive personalities in Scripture are shown displaying angry feelings without incurring God's displeasure. Consider how often David expresses anger in the midst of his most exalted statements of praise in the Psalms.

Or consider the encounter Jesus himself had with the fig tree (Mk 11:12-14, 11:20-21). Mark tells us that Jesus, being hungry, was annoyed because a certain fig tree had no fruit, even though there was a perfectly good reason for its barrenness: it wasn't the season of figs! Yet Jesus cursed the fig tree. Though many look for a higher spiritual meaning in this incident, the fact remains that Jesus went through a very real human emotional response in this case. We should take encouragement from this passage, for it gives us a basis for accepting the feelings of irritation we experience in aggravating incidents of daily life, such as getting stuck in traffic, or finding that an important file has been deleted on our computer at work.

I don't mean that merely accepting our feelings of anger guarantees we'll end up expressing them sensitively. We face a significant further challenge in learning to share our negative feelings in a way that's considerate to other people—that strengthens our bond with them rather than destroys it. Learning to give "I" messages rather than "you" messages, and to carefully think though the effect of what we say on others before we speak, can make an enormous difference.

Still, accepting our anger is a critical first step toward being able to share it in a constructive manner. When we feel guilty for being angry, we're more inclined to ignore our anger and let it fester. Outbursts are much more likely, which embarrass those around us and ourselves. Anger controls us before we have the chance to control it through a sensitive response.

Constructive Motivation from Anger

There is also a positive, even essential, side to anger. I doubt that we ever accomplish anything fruitful when anger isn't part of our motivation, on a certain level at least. My desire to write an article or book is fueled in part by discontent over how I believe an issue has been mistreated, and the unfortunate effect misconceptions have had on others. If you or I do anything to help someone else, or to improve our own life, it's because we're frustrated that certain needs (theirs or ours) are not being properly met. The anger we experience in such cases isn't hostility or outrage, but an energizing force that moves us to act constructively. It may be more of an underlying drive than an emotion on our "front burner." Still, it's a significant factor in our motivation.

I would like to hear more emphasis in Christian teaching upon this positive role of anger in motivating us (but without terming it righteous indignation).

Which brings me to a final point. If we can understand which situations cause us personally to feel this energizing sort of anger, we will gain a treasured insight into how God has fashioned our life. When our annoyance over a problem that we or others are facing is matched with the talent to remedy it, we have the potential to take one of the most redemptive steps we possibly can with our life. We each will do well to look carefully at how God may be inspiring us and guiding us through certain frustration that we feel.

Anger is not a sinful emotion but a human one. Dangerous? Yes, in the same way that energy itself is dangerous. But like any energy source, it can be channeled in a positive or harmful direction. Much of the key to dealing effectively with anger is learning to harness it and direct it in ways that glorify Christ and reflect his best intentions for our life.

6

If I Don't Express My Anger, Will I Blow Up?

WHEN CLEANING OUT AN OLD DESK of my father's, I came across a priceless treasure. It was a letter he wrote in the summer of 1959 to the president of his country club. "Dear Stephen," it begins.

"I want to tell you about this incident, not just because it was irritating and embarrassing to me, but more importantly because it points up so graphically a situation I am sure you will want to know about."

Dad explains that he had authorized me to take a female friend to the club for dinner as his guest, and that her parents provided transportation. "They arrived around 6:00 to 6:30. They sat in the grill for over a half-hour without being able to get a

waiter to take an order. Blaine tells me that there were waiters standing around, that a couple of times one started to his
table with a glass of water, and then went off in another direction.

"I had equipped Blaine with a note authorizing charges to
me, and ample cash for tips—plus instruction for generous tip-
ping. . . . Finally he took his girl out to the snack bar at the
swimming pool and bought hamburgers."

Dad, as it turns out, is just getting warmed up. My being
ignored as a young teenager in the grill was just the tip of the
iceberg. He goes on to say he has been frustrated personally
with the food service at times. "I have sat in the grill and twiddled
my thumbs while waiters gazed at the ceiling—then there is
always something wrong with the service, shortage of utensils,
errors or incomplete delivery of the order, etc. My last two experiences in entertaining important guests in the main dining
room were such that Dottie and I just don't feel that we can take
a chance any more."

Dad ruminates some more about these problems, then ends
page one noting, "We are just little folk, but how many free-
spending members are in a like frame of mind?"

We come now to the second of his epistle's two pages. Dad
mentions that the bowling alley manager treated him rudely
during a recent visit. He takes pains in the remainder of the
letter to affirm Stephen, and to commend him for doing a great
job in managing the club. The problem isn't Stephen's fault, he
stresses; incompetent employees are failing him.

Dad adds in some further banter, then concludes his tome
with a supportive admonition: "I hope you knock some heads
together in your kindly and gentle way."

The Challenge of Criticizing Constructively

I marveled at how well Dad had crafted this letter. His language is animated, his grammar excellent, his expression of thought very clear. The pages are impeccably typed, at a level of perfection that probably required several passes and the patience of Job to get right. He undoubtedly spent hours mulling over the content, then laying it down in a beautifully-typed document.

I marveled as well at how sensitively he expressed his complaints to the club president. Stephen was a good friend, and Dad had performed legal work for him for years. Dad was clearly concerned not to damage their friendship or professional relationship.

It impressed me greatly that, given his close friendship with Stephen, he didn't simply pick up the phone, call him and ventilate. Our tendency when we're perturbed is to do exactly that. We want to sound off immediately. We want to get it off our chest, to know we've been heard, to get feedback—and we want it all right away. Especially so, when our aggravation has been piqued, as in Dad's case. What dismayed him most was that my girlfriend's parents, who were members of a more prestigious club, now had a poor impression of his. The incident surely would reflect badly on him, our family and me.

"There is no way that I can make apology to the girl's family for the club's inhospitality," he laments.

Dad had a serious grievance. His temptation to phone Stephen at home that evening and complain must have been strong. Still, he had the good sense to collect himself, and then express his concerns diplomatically in a letter.

When we're frustrated, we always do best to take many deep breaths—to allow ourselves time to calm down and carefully think through our response. When we're seriously agitated with someone, it's often a good idea first to express our feelings in writing to them. Confronting them verbally poses the risk that we'll speak impulsively, then regret we can't "put the tooth-paste back in the tube." Putting our thoughts in writing allows us the leisure to weigh them and revise them, until we're certain we've communicated sensitively. It also allows the other person opportunity to measure their thoughts before responding, decreasing the chance an argument will suddenly spiral out of control.

Much of what made this letter such a wonderful find was the sense that life had served me up with a timeless lesson in how to confront someone constructively. It was inspiring to realize how seriously Dad had taken this challenge, and how skillfully he had carried it out.

On Second Thought . . .

But here's what touched me most. The letter was unmailed. What I had discovered filed away in that desk drawer wasn't a carbon or photocopy of Dad's letter to Stephen, but the original, folded inside a sealed envelope fully addressed. An uncanceled four-cent stamp was neatly pasted on the envelope.

Why did he choose at the last minute not to mail this treatise, over which he had obviously sweated for hours? I can only speculate. He may have feared that, in spite of his best efforts to be conciliatory, Stephen would still feel stung by his criticism and respond defensively. He may have worried that the letter would brand him at the club as a complainer. Or, on further reflection, he may have felt compassion for the service personnel—would Stephen overreact and fire workers who dearly needed the employment?

Whatever his reasons, Dad obviously concluded that more would be lost than gained by mailing the letter. It appears far-sightedness overruled his very strong urge to ventilate.

I thought immediately of a similar though much more notable incident from Lincoln's experience as president. Following the battle of Gettysburg in July 1863, Lee's defeated troops retreated southward, but found the Potomac River swollen from heavy rains and impassable. Lincoln ordered General Meade to attack Lee's army immediately and force them to surrender. Meade disobeyed Lincoln and called a council of war to deliberate the matter. While he procrastinated, the Potomac receded and Lee escaped.

Lincoln, boiling mad that Meade allowed a golden opportunity to entrap Lee and end the war slip away, wrote an angry letter to his general, expressing severe disappointment and bewilderment. Lincoln, though, never mailed the missive, which was discovered among his papers after he died.

Dale Carnegie cites this incident in his classic *How to Win Friends and Influence People*. He observes that the most effective leaders rarely criticize their associates—even when it's highly justified.

Criticism, Carnegie explains, seldom brings the positive outcome we expect. Denial runs so deep in most people that criticism fails to penetrate its shell. "Criticism is futile because it puts a person on the defensive and usually makes him strive to justify himself. Criticism is dangerous, because it wounds a person's precious pride, hurts his sense of importance, and arouses resentment."[1] He devotes his first chapter to expounding the point.

There is, of course, an irony in Carnegie's position. He makes his point by *criticizing*. He criticizes those who are critical, criticizes the belief that constructive criticism is usually constructive, and indirectly, at least, criticizes any of us who would disagree with him.

It's this irony that points out how impractical—and undesirable—it is to adopt an extreme position of never criticizing. There are jobs requiring it (what teacher can be effective without showing students where they need to grow?), occasions in family life and friendships when it's needed, and abusive situations where it's demanded. And we encounter those remarkable, magnanimous people, who not only benefit from our criticism, but even appreciate it (Prov. 17:10, 27:5-6).

Still, Carnegie has his point, which, given his folksy style, is better made by hyperbole when he first introduces it than by musing over exceptions. (And he does offer substantial advice later in his book about how to offer criticism sensitively, when it's truly necessary.) I agree with Carnegie at this point: *Most* of the time, when we believe someone will benefit from our criticism, or imagine we'll experience catharsis by getting it off our chest, we're mistaken. Far from helping the other person, our criticism hurts them and triggers their defenses. They become more entrenched in the position we wish to correct. And catharsis? Forget it. Even if an argument doesn't ensue, we feel dejected that our criticism didn't improve things, and wish we'd held our tongue.

The last state is *especially* likely to be worse than the first when our criticism is (a) unsolicited, (b) given in anger, (c) provided without a healthy dose of humility—where we point out that we also have serious faults and need the Lord's help just as greatly.

Even when given with substantial humility, we sometimes help someone more by not offering our critique. And even criticism that's solicited sometimes hurts more than edifies.

Jesus on Criticism's Boomerang Effect

Centuries before Carnegie preached his doctrine of not criticizing, Jesus urged similar constraint in a statement that surely stunned many listeners: "Judge not, that you be not judged" (Mt 7:1 RSV).

The judgment we express to someone else—or merely nurture in our heart—typically flies back in our face like sand thrown into approaching wind, Jesus says. By criticizing someone, we spur them to look more diligently for our faults, which they will surely find and expose. Jesus certainly implies a deeper principle here, too—that God is about the business of humbling those who seek to humble others.

His command also suggests a vital psychological insight. The fact that we're able to feel intensely critical of someone over some matter often indicates we're guilty of a similar offense. It's precisely because we know from personal experience how disabling this problem can be that we're able so quickly to identify it in someone else. Yet we find it far more comfortable to focus on the other's problem; *projection* is what psychologists call it today.

Jesus continues: "For with the judgment you pronounce you will be judged, and the measure you give will be the measure you get. Why do you see the speck that is in your brother's eye, but do not notice the log that is in your own eye? Or how can you say to your brother, 'Let me take the speck out of your eye,' when there is the log in your own eye? You hypocrite, first take the log out of your own eye, and then you will see clearly to take the speck out of your brother's eye" (Mt 7:2-5).

Jesus clearly intended the principle of not judging to be *pervasive* in the Christian life. His language is emphatic—*judge not*—almost as though he entertains no exceptions. Did he mean there is absolutely, positively never a time when we should criticize anyone? Clearly not, for he implies we'll sometimes need to address the "speck" in another's eye. Yet the emphasis in his imagery could not be plainer. We should focus primarily on our own problems, and require a strong burden of proof before approaching anyone else about theirs.

We must conclude from Jesus' teaching, too, that ventilation purely for its own sake is never justified. The likelihood is great it will be harmful—both to the person we rebuke and to ourselves.

Is Ventilation a Safety Valve?
But aren't we in danger of damaging our psychological health by not expressing our anger? Many psychologists believe so. According to ventilationist theories, pervasive in psychology for the past century, we *store* anger, and unless unleashed, it will grow and intensify, until we explode like Mount Vesuvius.

Carol Tavris debunks this notion in her insightful book *Anger: The Misunderstood Emotion.*[2] We don't store anger, Tavris points out, any more than we store positive emotions. Who would claim, for instance, that we'll explode if we don't express joy or gratitude? What's more, expressing anger—far from relieving it—often *nurtures* it, for by focusing on our angry feelings we intensify them. Expressing our anger, too, frequently sets up a chain of events that worsens the situation which has upset us, leaving us even more aggravated.

Anger is relieved, Tavris insists, not by its expression, but by the resolution of the problem provoking it.

Imagine, for instance, that a coworker informs you that she overheard your boss tell his secretary you're going to be fired. You've served this company faithfully and diligently for years. Besides, you've had a cordial relationship with your boss, who recently commended you highly for your work. You're outraged, not only that he'd think of terminating you, but that he'd be so duplicitous as to imply he's pleased with your work when he's actually intending to let you go.

For two weeks your resentment grows, and you barely sleep. Then comes the dreaded invitation to your boss's office. You sit stunned, as he explains that he intends to—*promote* you. Later, your coworker admits she must have misunderstood that conversation she overheard.

Now—what happens to your burning anger in that astonishing moment when you learn that you had things completely reversed? Why, it vanishes, of course. Yet if it's true that we store anger, it must still be there, still needing to be vented in some way. There's no mistaking, though, that it's gone—even though you haven't let it out at all. You have no more sensation of it than of physical pain that's suddenly relieved.

Each of us has endless experiences like this, where anger we've never expressed disappears in a moment, once the situation upsetting us is happily resolved. Reflecting on such episodes should convince us that we're not endangering our equilibrium by keeping the lid on angry feelings.

Whether expressing our anger relieves it depends upon the

results. Sometimes venting does improve things. The person we confront is contrite, and makes a sincere effort to address the problem that has perturbed us. We feel validated for being assertive. Our anger dissolves.

In many other cases we're severely disappointed with the outcome. The person we confront is defensive. Nothing improves. We're frustrated with ourselves for caving in to the urge to ventilate. Expressing our anger has magnified it.

The most redemptive thing we can do when we feel compelled to confront someone we're angry with is to consider as honestly as we can what the results will likely be. Are we confident that speaking our mind will help heal the situation? Then we should do so. If we're less than certain about the outcome, we should hold our peace.

Different Levels of Assertiveness

Even if we realize confronting someone may do more harm than good, we may still feel compelled to do so in order to preserve our integrity. Holding back is cowardly, we assume, and sends the wrong message. We need to be frank to stay properly assertive.

Yet a vital part of being assertive is owning our own life. We don't fully own our life if our well-being depends upon how others think about us or respond to us. If I feel it's necessary to tell someone off in order to save my pride, I'm letting that person have too much control over my life. My happiness is hinging too greatly on his needing to know I can stand up for myself, and upon my needing to affect him in a certain way. It's a higher form of assertiveness in this case to hold my tongue, especially if I know that speaking my mind is likely to undermine things further.

So often, too, the person we want to criticize is already well aware we're upset with them, and knows exactly what we want to say. They are braced for a confrontation, and ready with their best defense. The fact that we choose not to confront them may leave them surprised and grateful enough that they drop their defenses, and in humility take steps on their own initiative to address the problem that has angered us.

Tom Wolfe has observed that effective writing results as much from what writers leave out as from what they include. In the same way, we sometimes have greater influence on someone through what we don't say than through what we do. We're more effectively assertive by holding our peace.

I'm not suggesting we use silence as a *weapon*. If our motive in not confronting someone is to hurt them through our silence, then we're still allowing them to control our feelings too greatly. If we know that confronting someone isn't likely to help, then our goal should be to forgive this person. By letting go of animosity rather than ventilating it, we're not only acting graciously toward them, but doing ourselves an enormous favor as well—for we're removing any chance this person's action will continue to frustrate us. Indeed, forgiveness is the most supremely assertive step we can take.

I don't mean to downplay the challenge often involved in achieving genuine forgiveness. Yet it helps to know that by offering someone forgiveness we're not demonstrating weakness, but extraordinary character strength.

It helps, too, to know that the anger we're releasing will not remain secretly buried in some deep recess of our psyche, and come back later to haunt or damage us. At worst, we may feel a little embarrassed—that friends may think we're off our rocker for having let go of anger so successfully.

Or, that someone years from now may find and read that spirited letter we wrote and revised so carefully, then buried forever in our desk drawer.

7

Pearls of
Too Great a Price?

EVER SINCE READING John Steinbeck's *The Pearl* in high school, I've been haunted by a reflection of Juana early in the novel. After her husband, Kino, hauls a basket into their boat containing a bloated oyster with a mammoth pearl, Juana senses his excitement. Yet she pretends to look away. "It is not good to want a thing too much," she muses. "It sometimes drives the luck away. You must want it just enough, and you must be very tactful with God or the gods."[1]

In the story that follows, Juana's reflection becomes prophetic, as Kino's burning desire to turn the giant pearl into fortune destroys the simple but peaceful life they had enjoyed. The story's moral is blatant and chilling: it's dangerous to desire something too much, and often self-defeating.

Beyond her superstition about multiple gods, did Juana have

a handle on a principle of life that profoundly determines our own success or failure? Does wanting a benefit of life too greatly hinder our chance of obtaining it? Does God work against us when our desires grow too strong?

My study of Scripture has actually done more to convince me of the *importance* of desire than anything. Typically, far more is taught in Christian circles about the dangers of desire than its benefits. Yet Scripture has much to say about the positive—even essential—role of desire in human life, both as a motivator and as an indicator of God's guidance. We noted that when Paul declares in Philippians 2:13 that God *works* in us, the Greek verb literally translates "energizing." Paul is saying that God is *stimulating* us to do certain things with our life, through giving us certain desires that reflect his will.

Over a lifetime, most of us discover that we are most productive, and best relate to others for Christ, when we're doing work that we fundamentally enjoy.

Granted, certain desires are dangerous to us, even in small doses. The urge to experience a drug-induced high, or to pursue an affair with a married individual, will only lead to heartache and worse if we give in to it.

But what about the desire for otherwise wholesome benefits of life? Can the longing to develop a certain talent, to succeed in a particular career, to provide for my family, to be married or to marry a certain person, grow so strong that it contributes more to my failing than succeeding?

Self-Defeating Reactions

Let's set aside for a moment the question of whether God himself works against us in such cases, and look first at the human side. There is little question that we often shoot ourselves in the foot when desire grows too strong. One common reason is that, because we're so eager to gain a certain benefit, we may be too willing to make compromises or sacrifices that aren't truly necessary to our success. We may be too ready to sell ourselves short.

When desire is exorbitant, we're also more prone to nervous or impulsive reactions that hurt our chances of succeeding. Our neediness can work against us. When Kino realized he had found an extraordinary pearl, "he put back his head and howled. His eyes rolled up and he screamed and his body was rigid."[2] His exclamation caught the attention of other divers in the area, who quickly rowed to his canoe. News of his discovery soon spread like burning underbrush; pearl buyers schemed to defraud him, and robbers plotted to steal his prize. If Kino had merely kept his discovery to himself for a while, he would have avoided endless problems, and might have had time to come up with a reasonable strategy for selling the pearl. One impulsive reaction forever destroyed his bargaining edge.

In his book *You Can Negotiate Anything,* master negotiator Herb Cohen observes that in situations which require negotiation, we are usually at a disadvantage if we desire a result too greatly. It *is* important to care about the outcome, Cohen insists, but "not to care too much." When our heart is too fully in a matter, we often do better to let someone else handle the negotiating for us.[3]

Where Jacob Failed
We find an enlightening biblical example of Cohen's cardinal principle in the odyssey Jacob went through to win Rachel's hand in marriage (Gen 29:18-30). Jacob agreed to serve Rachel's

father, Laban, as a field laborer for seven years, in return for permission to marry Rachel afterward. Yet once Jacob had completed this period of service, Laban changed the terms. He gave Jacob his other daughter, Leah, to be his wife, then offered to give him Rachel also if he would serve Laban for another seven years.

What's stunning is that Jacob *agreed* to all of these terms, and as far as we know, never tried to challenge any of them. We might assume that such arrangements were simply traditional at that time. Yet when Abraham's servant had come to Laban's family previously, to seek a wife for Jacob's father, Isaac, Laban and his father agreed to let Laban's sister, Rebecca, return with the servant to marry Isaac *the following day* (Gen 24:50-51, 55-60). Abraham's servant secured a wife for Isaac from Laban's family without having to provide any labor in return. Nor was any service required from Isaac, Abraham or anyone for the prize of Rebecca.

Laban's family agreed so readily to let Rebecca go because they strongly desired for family members to marry within their extended blood family, and options were few and far between. This incentive was so high, in fact, that Jacob almost certainly could have negotiated much better terms for his own marriage to Rachel if he had tried.

Yet Jacob served Laban for fourteen years for Rachel, while no one served a single day for Rebecca. Why such an outlandish difference in terms?

The reason is that Abraham's servant—to use Herb Cohen's expression—cared, but did not care too much. He clearly wanted to succeed and please his master, yet neither his happiness nor his standing with Abraham *depended* upon his succeeding (Gen

24:7-8). Jacob, on the other hand, was crazed with desire for Rachel. He simply wasn't in a good state of mind to negotiate fairly for himself, and far too ready to accept the first arrangement offered to him.

Jacob's fatal flaw was that he *did* care too much. His love for Rachel was nothing short of an obsession. After she died, he developed a similar fixation on her first-born son, Joseph. Yet his exorbitant love for these two individuals set him up for extraordinary heartbreak when these relationships dropped out of his life.

From all the evidence we have, Jacob was not a truly happy person, particularly in his later years. Rachel's death, and Joseph's disappearance, left him chronically grief-stricken. Years later, when he was reunited with Joseph in Egypt, Jacob confessed to the Pharaoh that he had been depressed for much of his life (Gen 47:9).

Expecting the Best from God

Appreciating how Jacob's fixations rendered his life miserable allows us to address more meaningfully the question of whether God works against our reaching a goal when our desire becomes excessive. God is, emphatically, not against our succeeding. Nor is he against our happiness. The God of Scripture is not the capricious, prickly god of so much mythology, who must be appeased and petitioned tactfully if we are to gain what we want. God loves us infinitely more than we love ourselves! He desires the very best for us.

Which is just the point. *Because* God loves us and wants the best for us, he may refrain from granting a desire, if he knows that doing so would actually diminish our joy over the long term. Or he may wait beyond what we feel is a reasonable period to grant it, to allow us to grow to the point where we're better able to handle the benefits and responsibilities that the fulfillment of our desire entails.

God's concern is that, through it all, we develop character and understanding that help us realize his best for our life. The good news is that our desires play a critical role in helping us recognize his will. Long-term desires—especially those that have stood the test of time—often give us a vital window into what God wants us to do. God uses our desires to motivate us to take important steps with our life as well. Our most worthwhile accomplishments are usually stimulated by significant desire.

Helping Our Desires to Work for Us

Yet our desires, even for legitimate benefits of life, can become obsessive, as they did in Kino's case with the pearl, and Jacob's with Rachel and Joseph. How can we guard against this happening? How can we harvest desires that provide us with healthy motivation? And how can we make wise decisions based upon the ones we do experience? Here are some steps that can help:

• *Broaden your interests, diversify your affection.* Jacob wasn't wrong to love Rachel and Joseph, nor to love them deeply. Where he went wrong was in not diversifying his affection more. It appears that for a long time Rachel wasn't merely an important part of his life, but his entire reason for living. It doesn't seem that he had any vocational interests that strongly motivated him or any other significant friendships. I have to wonder if there was a treasure in Leah that Jacob never discovered, because her physical features weren't as appealing to him as Rachel's.

Most tragic was Jacob's fixation on Joseph. Jacob had many other children and, eventually, grandchildren. With the exception of Benjamin, though, there is no evidence he ever developed the bond with any of them that he enjoyed with Joseph. The results were tragic for both Jacob and his children.

One of the best steps we can take as a hedge against any one desire's becoming an unhealthy obsession is to have a variety of friendships and interests. As simple as the point sounds, it's easy to get stuck in the inertia of life and not broaden our contacts and interests as fully as we can. Each friendship we have enriches our life in unique ways, and most of us do well to have a number of them.

It helps us, too, to understand how resilient God has made us as humans. If one friendship or relationship fails, we can find another that provides as great support to us as the one we've lost. We'll look at this point more fully in chapter 10.

Each of us also has considerable potential for experiencing joy through being creative and productive. Here again, though, it's important to have more than one area of talent that we nurture.

I'll never forget an experience in 1972, when I was visiting Sterling Sound, a recording studio in New York City, to master a Sons of Thunder record. Following the session, I was standing on the sidewalk in front of the studio, chatting with a studio engineer who had helped us. A disheveled beggar walked up to us. I was stunned when the engineer embraced this man, greeted him warmly, and asked him about his family. He then stuffed a $20 bill in the beggar's shirt pocket as that man turned to walk away.

My engineer friend then explained to me that this ragged

man who had just approached us was once one of the most respected recording engineers in New York. Yet a fall had damaged his hearing, to the extent that he was no longer able to
produce quality recordings. Convinced he had no other meaningful options for his life, he resorted to begging.

This was one of the most tragic examples I've seen of
someone's staking their identity too greatly on one talent.

At the other, and more positive extreme, a friend told me
how he had helped an unemployed musician friend obtain a job
as a technical writer. The musician initially resisted the idea,
complaining that he was only qualified to perform music. He
knew nothing about the technical field my friend was encouraging him to pursue as a journalist. Yet my friend assured him
he could do it. He explained that you don't have to be an expert
in a field to write about it, but merely able to express information interestingly that others present to you. The musician agreed
to give it a try. He applied for the position and was hired. He has
done well in this job, and supported himself comfortably.

Like the musician, we each have areas of talent that are trans-
ferable—usually in far more ways than we realize. As we open
ourselves to new possibilities, we're often amazed at the doors
God opens for us.

• *Deepen your love for God.* The single greatest tragedy in
Jacob's life was that he never developed the close companion-
ship with God that his grandfather, Abraham, enjoyed. While
Jacob had some special encounters with God during his lifetime, they were very occasional. It doesn't seem that he ever
walked with God. And what relationship he did have with him
was mainly opportunistic (Gen 28:20-22).

Had Jacob enjoyed a growing friendship with God, he likely

would have kept his relationships with Rachel and Joseph in better perspective. Not only would he have had another, and greater, outlet for his affection, but he would have had God's counsel and encouragement to help him better order his life. And, undoubtedly, he would have drawn on God's strength more readily to move beyond his grief over losing Rachel and Joseph.

I never tire of repeating the cardinal advice of C. S. Lewis. Our problem, Lewis noted, isn't that we love things too much, but that we don't love God enough. If our attraction to some object of life is too strong, trying to reduce our affection for it will not help us as much as striving to increase our love for God.

Everything that we do to keep our relationship with Christ strong and growing contributes toward keeping our desires in healthy focus. The most encouraging part is that, as we open ourselves to Christ's influence, he works within us to fashion our desires. While some diminish, others grow stronger. The closer our walk with him becomes, the greater can be our confidence that our desires are reflecting his intentions for our life, and motivating us in the best possible way.

• *Be patient.* When a desire takes on too much importance, usually part of the problem is that we feel it must be met too urgently. The more we can learn the art of patience, the better we'll ensure that our dreams won't get out of hand.

The most important secret to patience is learning that our experience of joy can actually increase through delaying gratification. We are happiest when we have something to look forward to—even if it's a dream on the distant horizon. Hope is central to our happiness, as well as to our health and vitality.

Here, ironically, Jacob has something important to teach us. He did understand the dynamics of patience well. It's hard, in fact, to find a more inspiring example of patience in Scripture than Jacob's. He waited *seven years* for Rachel's hand, then agreed to work another seven. Waiting to marry her not only meant delaying sexual intimacy, but postponing friendship on other levels as well. Yet Jacob wasn't just willing to make this sacrifice of time, but *comfortable* doing so. He was so gifted at owning his desire as a *future* hope, that the period of waiting "seemed like only a few days to him because of his love for her" (Gen 29:20).

Laban shouldn't have required Jacob to labor so long for Rachel, and Jacob certainly could have negotiated better terms. Yet his patience in waiting for her is impressive in itself. Where he went wrong was in fixating too much on this future hope alone and not seeking additional outlets for his affection. If we can combine patience with broadening our interests, diversifying our affection, and deepening our love for God, this combination of steps will serve us well. It will help us to stay encouraged, while less tempted to devote more affection to any one area of life than it deserves.

• ***Be open to options where your desire is moderate rather than extreme.*** There is another step that helps us considerably. One of the best-kept secrets of happiness is that our greatest joy is often found in choosing alternatives where our attraction is moderate rather than extreme.

Many find they are happiest in a marriage where their romantic attraction to the other is significant but not volcanic. In this case, they're able to enjoy the benefits of the marriage, yet still have a life apart from it. And because their neediness is not as great as it would be if attraction were overwhelming, they're better able to give themselves to their spouse compassionately, and to sacrifice their own interests for the sake of their partner's.

Best of all, their affection has a chance to grow, since it's not already at full throttle. Many discover that over the years their attraction to their partner increases, and they feel more "in love" after ten or twenty years together than when they first married. When romantic love is extreme at the start of a marriage, one is often in for a letdown, as one discovers that the other person cannot possibly live up to his or her monumental expectations.

I realize that what I'm saying flies in the face of the popular Christian idea that you should "only marry someone whom you can't possibly live without." Ironically, most of us would find that if we did marry someone we couldn't live without, we'd be miserable. Our well-being would constantly rise and fall depending upon how well we felt he or she was meeting our needs. And this person, rather than merely being someone whom we cherish as a gift of God, would *become* our God.

Many major life choices work best when we base them upon moderate rather than extreme attraction. I'm not suggesting we should sell short important life dreams that we've long held. Nor should we compromise them. Yet sometimes we do need to *renegotiate* them. This is necessary because our ideals so often have sprung from a mix of healthy and unhealthy influences.

In life's real time it often works like this: God's best options for our life seem good to us, but less than perfect. The most encouraging part is that we don't always have to wait for situations to perfectly match our ideals before taking important steps with our life. Especially when trusted friends with good judgment feel that an alternative is right for us, we may do best to choose it, even though our attraction to it is only moderate. Many find that over time such a step of faith positions them to enjoy blessings that greatly exceed their initial expectations. Not a few find they have stumbled upon a pearl of great price.

8

Welcome Guidance from Unwelcome Circumstances

IN THE MID-1970S, I SERVED as a pastor on the staff of a St. Louis church for several years. The experience was a milestone for me. The senior pastor and congregation were highly supportive, and I grew in many important ways.

Yet I was often frustrated by the nature of pastoral work itself. Pastors are expected to be generalists—wearing many hats and responding to many emergencies. Many pastors thrive on this multifaceted aspect of church work and love the adventure of countless responsibilities, and I'm grateful for their natural devotion to this vital role. I found myself wanting to concentrate more on certain areas of ministry that utilized my gifts, and was often discouraged at how little time I had for these activities. The experience brought me face to face with the fact that, while I greatly enjoy challenging work, I prefer to focus on a few things and do them well.

That insight was invaluable, and it led me to begin an independent ministry. My work since then as a "resource pastor," with its focus on teaching and writing, has fit me amazingly well, and I've never regretted making this change. Yet I can't imagine I would have found the insight to do it, nor the motivation, had I not experienced some significant frustration as a pastor, which convinced me I was trying too hard to fit myself into an unnatural role. God, I believe, used the unwelcome aspects of pastoral work as much as the enjoyable to clarify this new direction I should take.

This positive role of frustration in my decision to launch Nehemiah Ministries is a good example of what human potential writer W. Clement Stone terms "inspirational dissatisfaction." Stone presents this concept in *The Success System That Never Fails*, which I read about twelve years ago.[1] This book, ironically, had sat on my shelf ignored for more than thirty years, and it would have helped me if I had read it when I was a pastor. Someone gave it to me in the late 1960s—so long ago that I can't remember who, nor whether it was a gift or a loan (undoubtedly the latter). I shied away from reading it all that time due to its title, which seemed audacious.

Then one afternoon in the summer of 2000, I had some free time and wanted to read something upbeat. I decided to give Stone's book a chance. It was, well, better than I expected. I found his notion of inspirational dissatisfaction, which he explores throughout the book, remarkably helpful, and I marveled that I'd never encountered it before.

Inspirational dissatisfaction, as Stone uses the term, is the positive role that our experiences of frustration play—both in helping us understand important steps we should take with our life, and in finding the motivation to take them. We may be unhappy in our job, for instance, because the work doesn't fit us well, or because coworkers aren't supportive or have unreasonable expectations of us. Frustration can be our ally in such cases—a red-alert that we need to seek a change.

I love this concept, as simple as it is, for it provides us a basis for seeing a silver lining in adverse circumstances, which we can easily miss. Some Christians view all frustrating situations fatalistically and hopelessly. They assume God is punishing them through these circumstances and that they shouldn't strive to change them.

On a more healthy level, we may recognize how such situations help us grow, but assume the silver lining comes only if we stay in them and allow God to stretch us there. That conclusion *is* often justified, and we can be too quick to run away from challenges, to say the least. Yet Scripture gives about equal weight to the other possibility—that God may use our frustration in such cases to enlighten us to the fact that we're not where we should be. Healthy thinking requires that we give fair consideration to both possibilities, and feel permission to think in both directions.

Unfortunately, our Christian teaching usually gives far more attention to the former possibility than the latter. We also have elaborate vocabulary for talking about the one ("pick up your cross," "accept your lot," "be a living sacrifice," "lose your life in order to find it"), and little in the way of convenient language to speak of the possibility that an unwelcome situation simply isn't right for us.

"Inspirational dissatisfaction" fills this gap wonderfully well and can make a redemptive contribution to our Christian vocabulary. We shouldn't underestimate the role that terminology plays in our ability to reason effectively and make sound decisions, given the extraordinary level of "self-talk" that we engage in constantly. I agonized over the question of whether to leave conventional church work for a specialized ministry far more than I should have, due especially to guilt-ridden self-talk. Simply knowing it was *permissible* to think in terms of inspirational dissatisfaction, and having that term available, would have made a big difference.

Turning Failure into Success

Stone notes another way in which inspirational dissatisfaction can function to our benefit. The discontent we feel over our own poor performance or behavior in some area can provide potent motivation to improve. Here again I find the concept helpful. Our tendency, when we're disappointed with ourselves, is to beat ourselves up and grow even more discouraged. Yet this discontent can provide the most powerful incentive we ever experience for positive change.

The most important turning point of my teenage years occurred when, one afternoon, alone in my father's home office, I suddenly felt such disgust over my poor performance in high school that I resolved to do better from that point forward. Surprisingly, that resolution stuck, and I worked hard at my coursework for the rest of my senior year, then throughout college and two graduate programs. The reason this resolution was so effective, while many others I had made failed, was due, I'm certain, to the *degree* of frustration I felt with myself at the time that I made it.

It's in this sense that psychologists often talk about the value of "hitting bottom" as a stimulus for change. Our discouragement doesn't *have* to reach this level to provide useful inspirational dissatisfaction. It can happen anytime we're disappointed with ourselves, if we're open to the possibility. Simply being aware of how frustration with ourselves can inspire positive change—and having a term for this dynamic—greatly enhances our ability to think optimistically. We're less likely to condemn ourselves for past mistakes and more likely to draw benefits from them.

Instead of wallowing in discouragement over how a thoughtless remark I made may have hurt someone, for instance, I can find the incentive to learn from the episode how to avoid such impulsive speaking in the future. I'm more likely to find the heart to apologize to this person as well.

Inspirational Dissatisfaction in Scripture

It's in weighing the significance of our frustration in unwelcome situations where we're likely to find the concept of inspirational dissatisfaction helpful most often, though, for our confusion over God's will is often greatest then. It's important to know that our discontent is sometimes his signal to seek a change. When we look for it in Scripture, we find many examples where this was the case.

One involves some disciples of Elisha, who find that their work and living conditions are too confining (2 Ki 6:1-7). They explain to him, "Look, the place where we meet with you is too small for us. Let us go to the Jordan, where each of us can get a pole; and let us build a place there for us to live."

Elisha responds to them, "Go."

They press him further, "Won't you please come with your servants," and he replies, "I will," and goes with them.

What's reassuring about this incident is that Elisha *validates* the frustration his disciples feel. He doesn't imply that they're selfish for feeling it, nor suggest they should simply learn to live with their cramped quarters and make the best of them. Instead, he agrees to help them make a constructive change.

The passage is refreshing to consider in any circumstance of life—such as a job, living situation or ministry—where we're frustrated over factors that work against our using our gifts effectively. We're shown that God may be alerting us through our frustration to seek improvements or even a new venue. We're freed from our natural tendency to think that the Christian response must be solely to accept our lot, and we're given permission—even encouraged—to weigh other possibilities.

Another biblical example of inspirational dissatisfaction involves Abraham's inability to find a wife for Isaac among the women of Cana (Gen 24). Both he and Isaac were likely frustrated over this situation and had long been so.

Abraham, especially, had strong reason to think they should simply accept reality in this case and not try to change it. His uncanny experience of miracles gave him a reason to be passive. Isaac's birth in itself, when Abraham and Sarah were both very old, was testimony—and Isaac's life a constant reminder—that God could solve the most impossible problems supernaturally. Shouldn't Abraham assume that, if God wanted Isaac married, God would provide a spouse for his son without special effort on Abraham's part?

Yet in this case Abraham was spurred by his frustration to take initiative to solve the problem. He sent his servant to his hometown of Haran to search for a wife for Isaac. Abraham clearly believed he was honoring God and had his blessing in taking this step, for he spoke to his servant of the help God's angel would provide in the journey. The mission was successful. The servant returned with Rebecca, who became Isaac's wife, and, from all indications in Scripture, was an exemplary match for him.

This passage is deeply encouraging to consider if you want to be married but believe that factors in your life are hindering you from finding someone compatible. You may be in a job setting where the likelihood of meeting someone is poor, or in a church or fellowship where you've been stigmatized as a "perpetual single." Traditional Christian counsel is, don't try to change these situations but trust that if God wants you married, he'll make it happen in spite of the limits of your circumstances. If no one suitable comes along, assume that God wants you to stay single, and pray that he will take away your desire for marriage.

Abraham's example presents a different model. It shows that taking initiative to change your circumstances in such cases can be highly appropriate and honoring to Christ. And it suggests that God may be prompting you through your frustration to leave certain situations and to look for ones that improve your prospects for finding a spouse.

Getting the Signals Straight

Simply knowing it's okay to consider the possibility God is moving us through our frustration to leave or change an unwelcome situation is encouraging in itself. The concept of inspirational dissatisfaction is greatly reassuring. It deepens our alertness to a potential source of God's guidance, and increases the possibility that we'll recognize action he wants us to take to solve problems.

It doesn't answer all the questions, though. We still have the challenge of determining God's will for us in a given instance. How can we know with confidence whether God wants us to leave a frustrating situation or stay? When does he want us to take initiative to change our circumstances, and when does he wish to change us so that we can learn to handle them better? Here are some steps that can help us reach the right conclusion.

1. Give each situation a fair chance. Every job, educational program, relationship, fellowship situation—you name it—has plenty of dry periods. We must be careful not to think that God is prompting us through the first sign of disenchantment to look for greener pastures. Some situations—degree programs especially—require plodding through much uninspiring time in order to reap the long-range benefits. I came close to bailing out of my doctoral program about halfway through, but am forever grateful that an insightful counselor persuaded me to stick with it. Be certain you've given a situation a reasonable opportunity to prove itself before considering the possibility of leaving.

2. Take your temperament into account. It's particularly important to understand your own temperament in weighing questions of God's guidance. What is your track record for sticking with challenges? Do you tend to quit too easily? Do you instinctively fear commitment or feel anxious after committing to situations that at first you were convinced you needed and would enjoy? If so, you should be slow to read your uneasiness as guidance from God to move on. Be a good life coach to yourself, and require that you stay committed to the challenging situation long enough that you can say you've given it a reasonable chance, before considering other options.

You may be at the other extreme. You stay in situations that are unpleasant or unfruitful well beyond a reasonable point, perhaps out of stubbornness, perhaps because you feel guilty about leaving. You need to err on the side of "cutting yourself some rope." Go overboard a bit in considering inspirational dissatisfaction as a possibility, and in allowing yourself the freedom to act on it. For you, the concept can be an especially liberating one.

3. Understand why you feel uncomfortable. We may feel uneasy in certain situations due to anxiety problems we can overcome. We may be edgy about commitment itself. Two other common apprehensions, reaching phobic levels for many, are the fear of public speaking and the fear of air travel—and many jobs require both. The good news is that these fears can be conquered, and help in doing so is widely available. If our discomfort in a job or any circumstance stems from an unreasonable fear, we shouldn't bail out but ought to confront our anxiety and get the best help available in dealing with it. We shouldn't let our fear be a basis for turning away from an opportunity that otherwise fits us well.

Our discomfort, on the other hand, may result from the fact that a situation doesn't match us well. If we're being treated unkindly, our gifts aren't being respected, or others are constantly laying unreasonable expectations on us, we have good reason to consider new options. Our frustration in such cases may be the Lord's wake-up call to move on.

4. *Weigh your positive alternatives.* At the same time, it's important to consider not only what we're reacting against, but what positive options are available to us. We can be tempted to leave an imperfect situation out of restlessness or a grass-is-greener mentality, when in fact we don't have something better to take its place. There are some instances—abusive situations especially—when we should bail out anyway. Yet in many cases it's better not to leave unless we have a clear idea of where we're going.

The point is strategically important in employment situations, for we're usually in the best position to market ourselves for a new job while we're still employed. A good test of whether the Lord may be prompting us to quit a job that we dislike is whether we have a better opportunity available. There are exceptions. We might leave in order to take some intentional time off to reassess our life's direction, or to move to a region where our options are better, or to get further training that will improve our future prospects. The important thing is to have a clear strategy in mind that provides us with a positive alternative.

It can be a good litmus test in other frustrating situations not to opt out until we know for certain where we're opting in. Responding is generally a more trustworthy impulse than reacting.

5. *Don't minimize the value of prayer and others' counsel.* The timeworn principles forever apply. Praying earnestly for God's guidance and for openness to his will helps us in many ways—giving us clearer thinking, greater alertness to indications of his leading and a more natural inclination to do his will.

Prayer is especially important when it comes to weighing the significance of our frustration, and can help us considerably in reaching the right conclusions about it. "Is any one among you suffering? Let him pray," James counsels (Jas 5:13 RSV). While James obviously means we should pray for relief in an adverse situation, he certainly means we should ask for wisdom about what to do as well. He also assures us that such praying brings us great benefit: "If any of you lacks wisdom, let him ask God, who gives to all men generously and without reproaching, and it will be given him" (Jas 1:5 RSV).

Others' counsel is nearly as important in the biblical view. Throughout Scripture we often see God using the insightful counsel of one person to clarify the thinking of another (Prov 27:17). I can only imagine the relief Timothy must have felt when Paul consoled him, "Don't let anyone look down on you because you are young" (1 Tim 4:12). Timothy was experiencing age discrimination; because of his youth, others weren't supporting him as fully as they should have in his pastoral role. Paul assured him that he shouldn't view this uncomfortable situation as simply a cross to bear but should take steps to correct it!

In other cases, Paul challenged Timothy to work on changing himself in order to accommodate the challenges of his work. "Do not neglect the gift you have," Paul exhorted him on one occasion (1 Tim 4:14), on another telling him, "Rekindle the gift of God that is within you" (2 Tim 1:6 both RSV).

In the same way, God will use others' counsel to help us sort through both sides of the inspirational dissatisfaction issue, and to decide whether we should seek to change our circumstances or change ourselves. We ought to draw especially on the counsel of those who see our life dynamically and desire God's very best for us.

Seeing the Bigger Picture

The best news in what we're saying is that the most challenging situations we experience—those where we may be tempted to think that God's hand has turned against us—can be settings where we gain treasured insight into our potential and God's will for us, and where we gain motivation for change that may not come any other way. Realizing that our frustration can generate such inspiration and enlightenment strengthens our confidence that God has good purposes for us in unwelcome situations, and it deepens our hope that he has better things for us in the future. And it helps us find the courage to take important steps of faith.

Having a term to describe it really does help. The next time you're tempted to think that life has dealt you a rotten hand in some area, try thinking in terms of inspirational dissatisfaction, and see if doing so makes a difference.

9

The Peril of Despair

WHEN THE STOCK MARKET CRASHED in October 1987, Jake feared it meant the end of life as he knew it. He had pinned his financial hopes for retirement upon years of careful investing in securities.

Within a day, chest pains landed him in the hospital. The diagnosis: a heart attack. His body had caved in to the bad news along with his emotions.

Jake did recover, and, after a long hospital stay, returned home and lived another eight years. The stock market gradually recovered as well, and Jake's holdings never plunged into the freefall he feared. Yet market ups and downs constantly unsettled him. He worried often that he hadn't set aside enough for retirement, and that a downturn would spell financial ruin for him and his wife.

Ironically, after he died at 83, his widow found that Jake's portfolio totaled over $700,000. He, unfortunately, had no orderly method for tracking its value, and most of his numerous stock and bond certificates were stuffed in a safe deposit drawer. He was thus left to ruminate about their actual worth, and often imagined the worst. In fact, he had more than enough to live comfortably, and about half his holdings were bonds, which don't typically lose their value during stock market declines.

A friend of his confided in me, "I just don't believe Jake had any idea how much he really had."

From this one picture of Jake, you might conclude he was simply a pessimist—unable by nature to see the glass half-full in his financial world. In fact, this Boston attorney would better be described as an optimist and positive thinker in most ways. Yet he could grow despondent under certain conditions, and was particularly vulnerable with his finances.

Facing Our Own Potential for Despair

Jake's experience with the stock market shows how even a basically optimistic person may despair under certain circumstances. It prods us each to look carefully at how we may be similarly inclined, and at how we can avoid such a plunge into clouded thinking.

Each of us has what psychologist Robert Bramson terms a potential for despair, which can be set in motion by various factors.[1] Yet we seldom recognize this tendency as a personality trait, let alone an unhealthy reaction. The result is that we normally don't think of it as something we can modify or control. Rather, we consider ourselves victims of despair when it occurs.

Yet despair by its very nature is almost always an overreaction, often severely so. We assume we're doomed to failure in a situation where we may still have plenty of reason for hope. Even worse, we may conclude from one setback that we're snakebitten, and that the bottom is falling out everywhere else in our life.

The potential for despair we each experience is also a uniquely personal one. What triggers despair varies greatly from person to person, and often has to do with our past. If we've been seriously slammed in some way, or know others who've been, we may inordinately fear the worst recurring in that area. We're shell-shocked, and it may take little to convince us that life is turning against us there.

Jake, born in 1912, was in his late teens and 20s when the Great Depression settled in. It broadsided for him what are usually one's most optimistic years. Seeing once-high-riding executives selling apples on Boston streets indelibly impressed him that financial catastrophe does occur, sometimes to the least expecting. Those years programmed him to fear the worst whenever stock market indications soured.

If we've likewise suffered a major tragedy or setback in our effort to reach a cherished goal, we may be predisposed to expect defeat if we try further. Even when our prospects are good, we perceive small setbacks as calamitous, a single failure proving the doors are forever bolted shut.

The Inertia Factor

The most unfortunate part of despair is that it's an emotion with inertia. Left unchecked, it takes on a life of its own. A case in point is the lame man in John 5, who lay by the pool of Bethesda.

He staked his hope for healing upon a popular belief—that when the pool rippled, an angel was present, and the first person into the water would be healed.

Yet he also regarded his situation as hopeless. "I have no man to put me into the pool when the water is troubled, and while I am going another steps down before me," he explained to Jesus. What's most stunning is that this man seemed to regard his dilemma as permanent; he had been ill for 38 years and "had been lying there a long time."

Jesus challenged his gloomy thinking, asking him, "Do you want to be healed?" By posing this question, Jesus suggested this man's attitude was working against his getting well. Yet he also implied that the man could break the inertia of his despair, and take steps toward healing.

The incident is a good one to keep in mind when we're facing a situation we think is hopeless. It challenges us to stop and consider whether our outlook itself is preventing us from seeing a solution. We're reminded that God gives us greater control to remedy the predicaments in our life than we tend to think. And Christ is on our side as we make the effort to see things more optimistically.

Winning the Fight

Fortunately, there's much we can do to stop our tumble into despair when it occurs, and to prevent it setting in, in the first place.

I'm not blandly suggesting the Christian never suffers defeat, nor has reason to feel discouraged. We suffer losses at times so severe that grief is the most appropriate reaction. Grief is healthy then, up to a point, and part of the healing process through which we come to terms with our loss.

But too often despair, as in Jake's case, is an extreme reaction, triggered more by the fear of calamity than the reality. And even when grief is appropriate, in response to a genuine loss, it can linger too long, and blind us to new beginnings and reasons for hope God provides us.

Here are some steps that can help us break the spell of unhealthy despair.

• ***Know yourself.*** Understanding our own psychology, and what makes us vulnerable to despair, helps us recognize how to avoid it.

Learn to identify despair as soon as it starts to set in, and to realize you're giving in to a deceptive emotion. Remember how your past predictions of doom have usually been wrong, and recall specific instances. Realize that your present fears are likely unreasonable as well, and take comfort in that. If you possibly can, laugh at your tendency to "catastrophize," which is only too human.

Think over your life, and recall instances when you've given in to despair. Identify the circumstances where you're vulnerable. If you know that certain situations tend to trigger despair, you can be braced for that happening when you have to face them. Being clearly aware what these circumstances are also allows you to choose to avoid them, if possible.

• ***Withhold judgment.*** Steve Simms, author of *Mindrobics: How to Be Happy the Rest of Your Life,*[2] offers this advice for times when life fails our expectations: *withhold judgment.* Take a deep breath. While he excepts obvious tragedies (a loved one's death, for instance), he insists we're usually on good ground not to negatively judge situations that disappoint us.

Simm's advice is sound wisdom. Most of our negative judgments are based on scant information; we don't know what's happening behind the scenes, nor how events will continue to unfold. Over time, we often find that setbacks have benefited us surprisingly. With the advantage of hindsight, we see them in a very different light. Given that, we do well, as a matter of principle, to resist judging them negatively, at least until sufficient time has passed.

• *Take inventory.* It's also very helpful simply to think as clearly and broadly as we can, both about the situation depressing us and our life in general. Despair results because we focus too much on one area—usually a setback or defeat we've suffered—to the exclusion of everything else.

Jake would have benefited from having an accounting system that allowed him to easily calculate his net worth. Merely being able to inventory his holdings would have let him see that his financial picture wasn't as bleak as he imagined. In the same way, taking inventory of a situation we're distressed about—looking at as many aspects as we can—often helps us see it more hopefully. In addition, we benefit from prodding our focus beyond this one problem to the other options we have, and the fuller picture of what God is doing in our life.

Most of us can use assistance in taking such inventory. Having a friend or counselor who views us positively, and is gifted in helping us see our life's bigger picture, helps immensely. We derive great benefit, too, from times of prayerful reflection, where we allow the Lord an unhindered opportunity to influence our thinking.

• *Shake off the dust.* But what about the more fundamental question of whether we should simply avoid certain circumstances? If we know a specific situation triggers our capacity for despair, should we try to stay clear of it altogether?

The answer depends upon God's purpose for us in the situation. Is it likely to help or hinder us in realizing our potential for Christ?

It is, of course, a prevailing theme of Scripture that God often is concerned not with changing the situation, but changing us. He brings many difficult circumstances into our life to help us grow. His concern is that we learn to handle challenges effectively and not be easily unsettled by adversity (Jas 1:2-4).

Yet, Scripture also has plenty to say about being good stewards of our life, and about managing it in ways that make us most productive for Christ. As we noted in the last chapter, this sometimes means responsibly deciding to leave a situation where we find it hard to be productive. One of the factors we must weigh is how we relate to the situation emotionally.

Again, it helps to remember that Jesus exhorted his disciples to leave towns that ungraciously received them, and to shake the dust off their feet as a testimony against the people (Mt 10:14, Mk 6:11, Lk 9:5, 10:11; see Acts 13:51). We might have expected him to encourage his disciples to be long-suffering then—to bear joyfully with those treating them poorly, and wait patiently for them to change. Yet he clearly intended his disciples to stay productive. I suspect, too, that he didn't want them to bog down emotionally in the inertia of unfruitful situations. He wanted them to stay as optimistic as possible about evangelizing, for in that spirit they'd most effectively minister.

The New Testament's most dramatic example of shaking off the dust is Paul's decision to switch his focus from the Jews to the Gentiles (Acts 18:6). Paul was extraordinarily attached to the Jews, and highly susceptible to discouragement when his efforts to convert them failed. He went so far as to write, "I speak the truth in Christ . . . I have great sorrow and unceasing anguish in my heart. For I could wish that I myself were cursed and cut off from Christ for the sake of my brothers, those of my own race, the people of Israel" (Rom 9:1-4). I suspect that part of God's purpose in shifting Paul to the Gentiles was to allow him to work in a more optimistic climate. While the Gentiles still offered him many challenges, he was more naturally resilient with them.

Paul's example shows us again that it's sometimes okay to leave or avoid a draining situation. The important question is how it contributes to realizing our potential in the long run. We ought to base our major commitments, as much as possible, upon how well an option fits our personality and gifts—including our natural ability to cope. By choosing major situations that match our temperament (career, job, church, relationships, hobbies, etc.), we're simply being good stewards of our life. Yet, as we've stressed, we'll need to adjust to many challenges within each of these settings, in order to reap the long-term benefits.

Jane, for example, is a highly-skilled journalist who loves writing more than any other field. Yet she takes even moderate editorial criticism hard, and rejection of a piece she's written crushes her. Jane shouldn't avoid a journalistic career because she's prone to these reactions, but should strive to modify them. Here, a counselor or support group can assist her invaluably in learning to take critiquing less personally.

At the same time, Jane should feel free to leave an unaffirming job for a more affirming one. Choosing one where people are supportive of her and her work, or leaving one where they're not, is simply exercising good stewardship.

• *Limit contact with negative people.* One point is abundantly clear from all of us: we should feel great freedom to limit our contact with highly negative people. Yes, Christ calls us to love and minister to those who are difficult to love, unquestionably. Yet he never expects us to be a doormat to anyone. If someone purposely is constantly insensitive or abusive to us, we shouldn't feel obliged to maintain any friendship with that person at all.

Many difficult people, to be sure, aren't intentionally unkind, and may even have their compassionate side. Still, their view of life is dour. We may feel that Christian love demands we spend time with them, for the sake of our positive influence. Yet we need to be honest about their influence upon us as well. If we find we're easily dragged into their pit of despair, we shouldn't place unrealistic burdens on ourselves. We may do best to limit our time with them to small doses, and to balance it by spending generous time with people who are positive about life—and about us.

• *Strengthen your trust in Christ.* Recently a friend invited me to visit an Alcoholics Anonymous meeting she regularly attends. It was my first chance to witness in person this program I've long admired from a distance.

Although I was familiar with AA proceedings and thought I knew what to expect, I was stunned by the humility these people displayed. Person after person spoke candidly about being powerless to remedy their problems apart from God's help.

The experience impressed me with how beneficial it is to face problems we have that are chronic. Yet how seldom we do.

As Christians, we're chronically inclined to lose the perspective of faith on our life. Yet usually we fail to appreciate just how recurrent the problem is.

Simply facing how perpetually our faith needs rekindling, is our single most important step toward keeping our heart encouraged in Christ. Nothing fights our slide into despair more effectively than grasping how fully he can be trusted—both with our present and our future. Yet we need to remind ourselves of this *constantly*, for faith that seems so vibrant one day eludes us the next. We need to return to this point again and again.

The great news is that, as we make this effort to refocus our attention on Christ, he always responds with what John calls "grace upon grace" (Jn 1:16 RSV)—that is, an endless supply of grace for our needs.

While our capacity for despair is considerable, our capacity for faith is even greater. In the effort to manage our emotions successfully, nothing is more important than striving to keep our faith strong. With vibrant faith, we'll be able to put setbacks in perspective, and keep our long-term aspirations strong. Here is the most important antidote to despair, and the greatest assurance that we'll stay open to the support and direction Christ wants to give us.

Appreciating the capacity for resilience God has given us also helps us greatly in dealing with despair. We'll look more closely at this benefit in the next chapter, and at how God has gifted us each with substantial ability to bounce back even from major losses. Indeed, appreciating this gift of resilience and allowing it to function is part of what genuine faith in Christ involves.

10

The Power of Resilience

ONE OF THE MOST HELPFUL insights we gain from studies of longevity is the importance of resilience. Centenarians, and others with exceptional life spans, are often those who are best able to accept loss and make new beginnings. Not that they don't feel the pain of major disappointments and grieve them profoundly. Still, the point comes when they are able to put the past behind them and move on. And they are remarkably adept at making fresh starts, even at unlikely points in life.

Jeanne Calment was a stunning example of this resilience. By the time she died in 1997 at 122, this Frenchwoman held the title of being the world's oldest living person with a documented birth date—a record still unbroken. Yet Calment suffered many misfortunes during her extraordinary lifetime. Pleurisy claimed her only child at 36, her husband died from eating tainted cherries at 72, and her only grandchild perished in a car accident at 36. After each crisis, though, she was able to regain her hope and "turn the page."

At 110 she gave up independent living and moved to a nursing home, where she continued to make new friends and adjust well to her new lifestyle. She never lost her positive outlook, even in her final years—or her sense of humor. On her 120th birthday a reporter asked what sort of future she envisioned. "A very brief one," Calment replied.

Genetics and lifestyle obviously played a role in Calment's unusual longevity. Yet her outlook on life was a critical factor as well.

During our own lifetime, we each experience a multitude of disappointments and setbacks. They range from minor aggravations (a friend forgets a lunch date, your favorite restaurant closes) to major unwelcome turns of fate (the breakup of a cherished relationship, the death of a loved one). The experience of loss is universal—none of us escapes it. Yet the way we respond to it varies greatly among us, and radically affects our quality of life.

Some people never fully recuperate from a major loss. They feel its pain for years or decades, and carry continual sorrow over the relationship that didn't work, the loved one who died unexpectedly, the dream that never succeeded. They had banked their hopes so strongly on this one area that life no longer has meaning without it. Grief for them becomes chronic.

At the other extreme are those with an uncanny ability to bounce back from disappointment. They may feel the pain of a loss acutely at first. But in time they always conclude that life still has important new horizons for them. They aren't afraid to

chance a new relationship or risk a new dream, and often succeed in forming deeply meaningful new attachments to people
and goals. Over time their life even becomes richer because of
their loss, for it deepens them in important ways.

The example of such people is so encouraging, for it helps
us see that it's possible to start over when life has knocked us
flat, and inspires us to try. We should reflect on the experience
of these people often, for their optimism is contagious.

Extremes in Scripture

We can also gain much by looking at individuals in the Bible,
and their responses to personal loss and tragedy. Scripture gives
enlightening examples at both extremes: we see those who over-
came the crush of a major loss successfully, and those who never
recovered.

Jacob was so demolished by the loss of a son that he never
regained his joy in living. Joseph was Jacob's favorite child,
being his beloved Rachel's first-born son. Jacob flaunted his
love for Joseph so blatantly that his brothers grew insanely jeal-
ous. One day when Joseph was sixteen, his brothers overpow-
ered him and sold him to slave traders, who carried him off to
Egypt. His brothers then soaked Joseph's coat in a dead animal's
blood and presented it to Jacob, suggesting Joseph was killed
by a wild beast.

Scripture minces no words in describing Jacob's grief as
torrential. He "tore his clothes, put on sackcloth and mourned
for his son many days. All his sons and daughters came to comfort him, but he refused to be comforted. 'No,' he said, 'I will
continue to mourn till I join my son in the grave.' So his father
wept for him" (Gen 37:34-35).

Jacob's anguish never relented, but became chronic. When he finally reunited with Joseph in Egypt many years later, he declared to the Pharaoh, "The years of my pilgrimage are a hundred and thirty. My years have been few and difficult, and they do not equal the years of the pilgrimage of my fathers" (Gen 47:9).

Jacob's initial grief over losing Joseph is only too understandable. Yet he fixated on his loss and never rebounded. Tragically, Jacob had many other children, yet never formed the intimate attachment with any that he enjoyed with Joseph— and apparently never tried. God surely gave Jacob numerous opportunities to pick up his life again, yet he remained blind to most of it.

The prophet Samuel is someone who responded to loss in a more dynamic and healthy manner. God called Samuel to establish Saul as Israel's first king, and Samuel took the responsibility deeply personally. He ached to see Saul become a mature spiritual leader, and Israel a nation that followed the Lord wholeheartedly in all its ways.

Saul failed miserably in this role, and God decided to remove him. The news devastated Samuel. He "was angry; and he cried to the Lord all night. . . . Samuel did not see Saul again until the day of his death, but Samuel grieved over Saul" (1 Sam 15:11, 35 RSV).

God allowed Samuel to mourn Saul's defeat for some time. But God finally confronted Samuel, telling him it was time to stop grieving and to devote his energies to a new task. "The Lord said to Samuel, 'How long will you grieve over Saul, seeing I have rejected him from being king over Israel? Fill your horn with oil, and go; I will send you to Jesse the Bethlehemite, for I have provided for myself a king among his sons'" (1 Sam 16:1 RSV).

Samuel had endured an excruciating defeat in Saul's downfall. Yet God still had important work for him to do. He was to recruit David and prepare him to become Israel's king. Fortunately, Samuel had the good sense to obey God and accept this new mission, even though it must have been hard to let go of his grief over Saul at first.

The fact that Samuel was able to move beyond his remorse and turn his attention to David brought benefit not only to himself and David, but to an entire nation. From the evidence we have, Samuel enjoyed working with David, friendship blossomed between them, and Samuel's interest in life and ministry revived. Samuel is an inspiring example of someone in Scripture who learned to turn the page.

Fresh Heart for Fresh Starts

Some people, as we've noted, are natural optimists. Their ability to see the bright side of a dark situation and reset their sights after disappointment is mystifying to the rest of us, who are flattened by the same misfortune. Most of us have to work at being optimistic. We have to take decisive steps to break the spell of despair, which can hold us captive for long periods. The challenge is greatest when we experience a serious loss. It can cast a dark shadow over our life from that point on, and forever color our perception of God's possibilities for us.

In reality, we are much more capable of rebounding from major setbacks than we normally imagine. And we have much greater control over the healing process than we typically think. Here are four steps that can help in recovering from a substantial loss.

• *Take time to grieve your loss.* Minor setbacks and daily annoyances are best sloughed off. But major misfortunes need to be grieved. Scripture could scarcely be clearer on the point. Hebrew tradition required mourning the death of a loved one for a substantial period—often thirty days—and godly people throughout the Bible took the principle seriously.

Well-meaning Christians sometimes teach that if our faith is strong enough, we'll remain positive through any adversity. Scripture, though, never bypasses the *process* through which we gain the outlook of faith. Grief is sometimes an essential step.

If you have suffered a difficult loss, allow yourself fair opportunity to recover emotionally. If you can take time off from other activities and focus exclusively on coming to terms with your loss, do so. Otherwise, reduce your workload as much as possible for a while. Be gentle on yourself, and don't expect to move mountains during this time. Give yourself a reasonable period to mourn your loss, to face the pain you feel and work through it.

• *Appreciate the resilience God has put within you.* At the same time, remember how capable God has made you of bouncing back from disappointment. He has built into each of us the ability to let go of past hurts and refocus our affection in new directions.

The failure to appreciate this fundamental fact of human nature can be tragic. We noted that the most common cause of teenage suicide is the first rejection in romance. The pain of losing at love is so overwhelming that a young person can't see beyond it, or imagine that romance will ever be possible again. In reality, I don't know any happily married person who didn't endure at least one heartbreaking rejection when single, and most have suffered at least several.

By the time most of us get married, we discover that it's possible not only to love again, but to leave the hurts of past rejections behind us as distant memories. We find that affection can be redirected in the area we might least expect—romantic love.

Resilience works this way in every area of life. Disappointments in friendship, career, church life, and reaching personal goals never have to be terminal blows. We can find new opportunities as fulfilling as the ones we've lost. We usually underestimate our potential for resilience, and need to remind ourselves often just how strong it is.

• *Dwell on God's healing nature.* We should also bring to mind constantly that it's central to God's nature to bring healing to our deepest hurts. God's role as a healer is one of Scripture's most pervasive themes. Jesus, as we've noted, spent more time during his earthly ministry healing physical and emotional problems than he did preaching doctrinal truth.

Jesus' miracles show God's healing through relief of symptoms. He also heals through changing circumstances and bringing fresh opportunities into our lives. This side of God's healing nature is displayed in countless examples in Scripture, as well as in many promises that God will compensate us for our hurts:

The LORD builds up Jerusalem; he gathers the outcasts of Israel. He heals the brokenhearted, and binds up their wounds. (Ps 147:2-3)

A father to the fatherless, a defender of widows, is God in his holy dwelling. God sets the lonely in families. (Ps 68:5-6)

> He gives the barren woman a home, making her the joyous mother of children. (Ps 113:9 RSV)

> Instead of your shame you will receive a double portion, and instead of disgrace you will rejoice in your inheritance. And so you will inherit a double portion in your land, and everlasting joy will be yours. (Is 61:7)

> Return to your fortress, you prisoners of hope; even now I announce that I will restore twice as much to you. (Zech 9:12)

> The LORD upholds all who are falling, and raises up all who are bowed down. (Ps 145:14 RSV)

We should dwell on passages like these whenever we feel that life has dealt us a rotten hand. It's too easy at such times to imagine that God has abandoned us. We need every reminder that he not only is hurting with us but, in time, will bring renewal. We ought to hold tight to this hope, as an article of faith, and take heart often that it's God's nature to heal by providing us with new beginnings.

• *Take bold steps to break the inertia.* After spending some time lamenting a loss, we need to take determined steps to break the spell of our grief. The point when we should do so often comes well before we *feel* ready. Yet the effect of even a small beginning can be surprisingly therapeutic. A single date following a broken romance may be enough to convince us that our feelings can heal, and that there's hope for our future in relationships.

Consider the Israelites' situation in Babylon as described in Jeremiah 29:4-7:

This is what the LORD Almighty, the God of Israel, says to all those I carried into exile from Jerusalem to Babylon: "Build houses and settle down; plant gardens and eat what they produce. Marry and have sons and daughters; find wives for your sons and give your daughters in marriage, so that they too may have sons and daughters. Increase in number there; do not decrease. Also, seek the peace and prosperity of the city to which I have carried you into exile. Pray to the LORD for it, because if it prospers, you too will prosper."

We would call these Israelites, who had been deported to Babylon, clinically depressed today. They had been mourning their homeland continually, seeing no good whatever in their present circumstances. But now God addresses them through Jeremiah, telling them they've grieved their deportation long enough. It's time to make the best of their new situation, as highly imperfect as it seems. They should take bold initiative to build homes, to be economically productive, to find spouses for themselves and their children, and raise families. Even though they feel far from ready, God tells them to do these things anyway, implying he'll provide many successes as they move ahead—for it's after instructing them in this way that he gives them one of the greatest assurances of Scripture: "'For I know the plans I have for you,' declares the LORD, 'plans to prosper you and not to harm you, plans to give you hope and a future'" (v. 11).

When the foundations of our life have been knocked out through a major disappointment or broken dream, we should remember the Israelites' experience in Babylon, and how God counseled them. Their example warns us that we can become so immersed in grief, and fixated on our loss, that we miss the special opportunities God gives us to rebuild our life. It can take courageous initiative to break the grip of our grief and make a fresh start. We should pray earnestly that God will help us understand when it is time to step forward, and that he'll give us courage to go ahead.

We may benefit, too, from the counsel of others, in deciding when and how to forge new beginnings.

Yet simply knowing God *wants* us to make them is encouraging in itself. It can make the difference in finding the heart to try.

11

Paranoia Can Annoy Ya

I KNEW IT SPELLED TROUBLE. Her voice trembled and was clearly stressed. Her message on my answering tape was abrupt: "Please call me back as soon as possible." She left her name and number, but no explanation why she called.

I didn't recognize her name. But the 253 prefix on her phone number meant she lived near us in Damascus. She didn't know Evie or me personally, it appeared, since she didn't ask for either of us by name. This can only mean one thing, I concluded: One of our boys has gotten into trouble, and she wants to give me an earful. They've damaged her property, and she wants me to pay.

Wanting to defuse the problem as quickly as possible, I phoned her back immediately, even though it was now 10:00 p.m. But I got her answering machine. Disappointed, I left my name and number, and told her to call me anytime.

When I awoke the next morning, I felt like a dark cloud was hanging over the day. I'm going to have to engage in a difficult conversation with this woman, I mused. That thought nagged me all morning, and then all afternoon, as I anxiously awaited her call. Why was she taking so long to call back?

Finally, around 5:00 p.m., she phoned. I recognized her voice immediately and braced for a confrontation. To my surprise, she asked why *I* had phoned *her.* "I was returning your message," I explained, "which I assume concerns one of my boys," and I mentioned their names. "I don't know either of your sons or you," she replied. "I must have dialed your number by mistake."

Curious how this could have happened, I asked if she had been looking for a pastor in the phone directory, and picked my name at random. "No," she answered, "but I could sure use a pastor right now—my life is a mess!"

Oh.

In just several minutes, my perception of this woman and why she had phoned me turned completely around. She not only wasn't angry with me or anyone in my family—but hadn't been thinking about us at all! And far from wanting to scold me, she was immersed in her own problems and wanted encouragement. I had misread the cues at every point.

Although the incident took place some years ago, I well remember how I let an imaginary problem ruin my day. I could cite so many examples like it, where I found that my suspicions of what someone was thinking contrasted strongly with reality. My guess is that you can supply plenty of examples of your own. We so easily misinterpret others' negative feelings, and make ourselves miserable in the process.

A Common Mistake

We've all had the experience, probably more often than we like to admit. We've sensed that someone was angry or hurt, then worried ourselves sick about what they were thinking. We assumed they were angry *at us,* intent on confronting us or hurting us. In time, we found that we hadn't a clue about what they were really thinking. Their anguish wasn't directed at us at all, but toward their own pressing problems. They may even have welcomed our encouragement and listening ear.

When it comes to imagining what others think of us, it's easy to fall into a pattern of expecting the worst. *Paranoia* is what we often call it lightheartedly today. This is our popular adaptation of the psychiatric term, of course. Clinical paranoia is a serious psychological problem. True paranoids are pathologically suspicious of others' motives. Many suffer psychotic delusions about being watched or persecuted.

Most of us are not about to join a local militia to defend ourselves against "the encroaching evil forces of government." Nor do we imagine that aliens have implanted listening devices in our ears. Yet we do spend considerable energy worrying about what others think of us. We may instinctively assume that others don't like us, even when no evidence suggests this is true. Harboring such suspicions is a serious enough problem for many of us, that it helps us to have a word for it—even if we use that term somewhat tongue-in-cheek.

The tragedy is that even this "normal" paranoia can hinder us from realizing our potential for Christ and experiencing his abundant life. Our negative assumptions about what others think can cause us to expect failure at points where God intends us to succeed. We may fail to recognize golden opportunities he's presenting to us, in relationships, career and other areas. We need to recognize this mentality for what it is. And we need to take steps to ensure that it doesn't become a controlling factor in our life.

Paranoia in Scripture

We don't find the word "paranoia" or any equivalent in Scripture. Yet there are plenty of examples, both of the extreme problem and of the more common apprehensions we all experience. We see true paranoids: Laban, the father of Rebecca; Pharaoh, king of Egypt during the Exodus; Saul, Ahab, and other Old Testament kings; Haman, the king's friend in the book of Esther; and Herod, king of Israel at the time of Jesus' birth. Each of these men worried pathologically about others' motives and intentions. Paranoiac obsession led some of them to commit heinous acts. Fear that Jesus would dethrone him, for example, impelled Herod to order all babies in Bethlehem murdered, in a frantic effort to find and kill the newborn Jesus.

Yet we also see many examples in the Bible of godly individuals worrying unnecessarily about being hurt or rejected by others. Moses is a prime example. When he was forty, he killed an Egyptian whom he caught abusing a Jew. Fear of retaliation from the incident led Moses to seek refuge in the desert of Midian. While his fear was justified at first, he remained in seclusion there for *forty years*—long beyond the point when he likely faced any real danger in Egypt.

Throughout his time in Midian, Moses lived greatly beneath his potential, and the Israelites in Egypt were deprived of his gift of passionate leadership. He developed such deep inferiority that when God finally appeared to him in a burning bush, and told him explicitly to deliver Israel, Moses could only imagine failure and rejection. Even though God assured him emphatically that he would succeed, Moses declared, "But behold, they will not believe me or listen to my voice, for they will say, 'The LORD did not appear to you'" (Ex 4:1 RSV).

In addition to his dread of being killed if he returned to Egypt, Moses feared that others would be repelled by his speaking style, which he perceived as hesitant and stuttering. He was certain also that the Jews would regard him as an impostor, and not find his account of God's appearing to him credible. These assumptions would have kept him locked in place, were it not for God's going to exceptional lengths to prod him forward.

When Moses did venture forth and speak to the Israelites, of course, their response was radically different than he anticipated. His negative expectations were shattered. It's expressed in one of the most beautifully ironic statements in Scripture: "And the people believed; and when they heard that the LORD had visited the people of Israel and that he had seen their affliction, they bowed their heads and worshiped" (Ex 4:31 RSV).

It is to Moses' credit that he found the resolve to respond to God's call and return to Egypt, in spite of his extreme inhibitions. Yet if God hadn't confronted him so dramatically, he never would have broken the inertia. We're reminded how easily paranoid thinking can blind us to good opportunities, and keep us from the best God desires for us.

Letting Go of Paranoia

Fortunately, there is much we can do to address the problem. Clinical paranoia, to be sure, is a debilitating condition that always requires professional help. Yet the normal fears we all experience, about others not liking us or wanting to harm us, are a different story. They can often be dealt with through certain practical steps to change our outlook. Here are some suggestions that can help.

• *Face your concerns honestly in prayer, and reaffirm your faith in Christ.* The impact of paranoid feelings can be reduced greatly through prayer. This is one of the most important lessons of the psalms.

Our worries about others not liking us or rejecting us are mild compared to the apprehensions David expresses in many of his psalms. He fills them with ruminations about the evil designs of his enemies—sometimes even of his friends. As Israel's chief political leader, of course, David had many real enemies and faced plenty of legitimate threats from them. Yet in spite of his spiritual maturity, he was anything but unruffled by their plans. The psalms depict a deeply human side of David, and show that he spent considerable time and energy brooding about the malicious intentions of others. For instance:

My enemies say of me in malice,
     "When will he die and his name perish?"
When one of them comes to see me,
     he speaks falsely, while his heart gathers slander;
     then he goes out and spreads it around.
All my enemies whisper together against me;
     they imagine the worst for me, saying,
"A vile disease has afflicted him;
     he will never get up from the place where he lies."
Even my close friend,
     someone I trusted,

one who shared my bread,

has turned against me. (Ps 41:5-9)

It is comforting to find this psalm revealing David's humanity so graphically. We can take heart from his example that we're not psychologically imbalanced just because we're preoccupied with what others think about us. David often was, even though his relationship with God was strong, and he is one of Scripture's most impressive role models. The apprehensions he expresses in this psalm are also more intense than those we often experience. We may rest assured that our typical fears about others mistreating us are normal and human.

David's example is equally encouraging in showing us the freedom we should feel to express our concerns to God honestly in prayer. David states his frustrations pointedly to God in this psalm, clearly feeling comfortable doing so. He shows that we don't have to mince words when voicing our anxieties to God. If we fear animosity from someone, we can tell God so and tell him explicitly, no matter how far-fetched our apprehensions may be.

Yet David did more than simply ventilate by praying in this fashion. He went a vital step further, affirming that he trusted God in spite of his fears. He concludes his psalm by declaring,

I know that you are pleased with me,

for my enemy does not triumph over me.

Because of my integrity you uphold me

and set me in your presence forever.

Praise be to the LORD, the God of Israel,

from everlasting to everlasting.

Amen and Amen. (Ps 41:11-13)

Here we discover the major benefit of prayer for David. Through it he was able to regain his confidence in the Lord and put his fears in right perspective. We find David following this pattern of expressing aggravation, then reaffirming his faith, in psalm after psalm.

Prayer can help us similarly when we fall into paranoid thinking. Following David's example, we should begin by detailing our concerns frankly to God. Yet we shouldn't stop there. We should then call to mind those facts about God and his care for us that bring us greatest comfort. We should remind ourselves of his promises—to protect us, to provide for us abundantly, and to work out an ideal plan for our life. We should dwell on assurances like these, and then in prayer, reaffirm our convictions about them. Following this approach gives God the best opportunity to strengthen our faith, calm our fears, and help us understand where our anxieties are misplaced.

Christ extends far more grace and healing to us through this process of prayer than we normally imagine. Its therapeutic value in helping us break the grip of fear is immense.

• *Check your thinking.* Whenever we catch ourselves worrying about others being against us, we should stop and check our thinking. Is there really any reasonable basis for our fear? Or is it more likely that we're giving way to paranoid thinking out of habit? It can help us to recall similar situations in the past when our suspicions proved mistaken. The lesson of that phone call is one I've never forgotten.

We will benefit greatly by making a habit of examining our thinking and questioning our negative assumptions. If we tend to be pessimistic in general, it's a good rule of thumb that our conclusions are too gloomy—and we can take encouragement from knowing that. With practice, we can learn to stay more tentative in what we assume others are thinking about us, and not instinctively to expect the worst.

• *Practice optimism.* We noted in chapter two that Ronald Reagan's remarkable success with people was due to his personal expectations. He always assumed everyone he encountered would like him. As president, Reagan maintained surprisingly good relationships with many political enemies.

Should we strive for such unshakable confidence personally? Well . . . if I had to choose between the extremes—between assuming everyone likes me or everyone hates me—I'd choose the former. It's closer to a healthy attitude about relationships, and our expectations so often become self-fulfilling prophecies.

Most of us, though, simply aren't capable of such extreme positive thinking. Besides, it's a denial of reality. None of us, no matter how likable, will succeed in every effort we make to relate to others. We'll experience rejection and difficult encounters from time to time. Still, there is an outlook of optimism that's appropriate for us as Christians, and that will contribute to our success with people.

We may be confident that God desires the very best for us, and is working for our good in countless ways "behind the scenes." We may also be assured that he desires us to enjoy significant success with people, and is extending his help and healing to us in this area. To worry incessantly that others are against us is a denial both of God's love for us and of his redemptive influence in others' lives. We're on better ground to assume he is bringing about encouraging developments in the situations that concern us, and to stay hopeful for happy outcomes.

We may be certain, too, that if we do have a difficult encounter with someone, God will provide us the grace to handle it. Since we can never predict exactly *how* God will extend grace before it happens, it's pointless to worry ourselves sick about the specifics. We can simply trust that he will help us at the moment we need it, and help us substantially.

Another important principle of optimism is to strive to view bad experiences as aberrations rather than the norm—the point we stressed in chapter three. Too often we do the opposite. In our discouragement over someone's insensitivity, we assume that others are equally upset with us and will also be treating us unkindly. As our anxieties fester, we begin imagining that God is angry with us, and punishing us by arousing others against us. Such is the way our ruminations grow, as we reason "from the specific to the general."

If an unwelcome encounter with someone offers clear lessons, we should learn and benefit from it. But we shouldn't assume it signifies a pattern of fallout in our other relationships. And in no case should we conclude that God's hand has turned against us. To the contrary, we should call to mind promises of Scripture which assure us that God gives special grace to us in difficult times. "You are my fortress, my refuge in times of trouble" (Ps 59:16; see also Ps 9:9, 27:5, 32:7, 41:1, 46:1, 50:15, 91:15, 107:6, 138:7).

With time and practice, we can learn to focus our thinking in such optimistic directions. We should remind ourselves of these principles often, and call them to mind whenever our worries about others' intentions get out of hand.

• ***Sharpen your people skills.*** There's a further step that helps greatly to reduce feelings of paranoia. We each have far more ability to defuse others' negative feelings toward us than we usually assume. What if we're right?—someone *is* angry or frustrated with us. This doesn't mean that we're powerless to do anything to remedy the problem. This person may be more open to talking things through than we think. A sensitive, affirming response to them may do wonders to change their feelings and resolve the matter.

Anything we do to improve our skills with people will reduce our tendency to worry about what they think, for we'll be confident we can handle problems that arise. It's the belief that we're helpless in dealing with people that makes us prone to obsess about difficult encounters occurring. Taking a seminar or reading a book on sharpening social skills can help; counseling may benefit us as well. As our confidence with people increases, our anxieties concerning them will diminish—in some cases dramatically.

• *Move ahead in spite of your fears.* In my work with Nehemiah Ministries, I've often spoken to Christian groups whose theological convictions differ from mine at certain points. In the early period of this ministry, I dreaded these situations, fearing confrontations would occur. They seldom did. In fact, in more than thirty years of conference speaking and lecturing, I've usually found that those who disagree with me are gracious, not mean-spirited. Time and again, I've also found that speaking events which I've expected to be the most challenging have been the ones where ministry most obviously seems to have occurred.

Through these events, I've grown comfortable speaking to diverse groups, and now am inclined to expect the best and not the worst. Yet it's taken time and—especially—*experience* to reach this point. No amount of study or reflection would have changed my perspective, without my encountering these situations that I feared would be difficult.

The most common fallacy people have about conquering fear, phobia experts point out, is that we can overcome our apprehensions just by changing our outlook—in advance, before we actually do the thing that frightens us. It never works that way. We can make *some* progress by working on our thinking. Yet facing the situation we fear is essential to finally putting our anxieties to rest.

This principle applies not only to conquering phobias but to overcoming any inhibition. Paranoid assumptions that trouble us are not likely to disappear fully until we step into the social situations we fear, and discover firsthand that our concerns are unfounded.

We spend far too much energy imagining unpleasant encounters that never occur. Too often our gloomy expectations keep us from taking important steps of faith. Through prayer and careful reflection, we can begin to change our patterns of thinking, and reshape our expectations into more optimistic ones. God may extend special healing to us as well. Yet we shouldn't assume that all apprehension must vanish before we go ahead and do what is challenging to us. Moving forward in spite of our inhibitions will be necessary, both to realize our potential for Christ and to master our fears.

I'm speaking of such practical steps as:
- *Phoning for the date*
- *Requesting the job interview*
- *Seeking an improvement in our job*
- *Asking for forgiveness*
- *Sharing our faith with someone who needs to hear about*

Christ
- *Throwing the party at our home*
- *Asking someone to help us with a special need*
- *Visiting the church or Sunday school class.*

Through the strength Christ gives us, we can find the courage to stare fear down and take steps like these—and open ourselves to the fullest blessings of God.

12

The Positive Side of Mixed Emotions

"I'M THIRTY YEARS OLD AND have been married four years," James explained to Dr. Lawrence.

"Some days I feel ecstatic to be married to Sarah. But other days the spark isn't as strong.

"There's no question about my commitment. I'm resolved to stay faithful to her and the marriage no matter how much my feelings fluctuate. But I wish they'd grow more consistently positive; these mixed emotions are driving me nuts.

"Here's the weirdest part," he continued. "Most of the time I have mixed emotions about marriage itself. I'm delighted to finally be married and grateful for its many benefits. Yet I also long for certain freedoms I enjoyed as a single man. And these mixed feelings go on within me at the same time. Recently a friend called my attitude schizophrenic, and that got me worried. I decided it was time to talk with a counselor."

Dr. Lawrence gave James some practical advice he found helpful. "Take five or ten minutes at the beginning of each day, and think about occasions when you have felt most in love with Sarah and most excited she is your wife. Focus on those things that most attracted you to her in the first place. Enjoy the bliss of those memories for a moment, and then recall them many times during the day. Bring to mind also the benefits of marriage that are most important to you, and rehearse them many times throughout the day. Practicing these simple steps daily will help your attraction to Sarah and the marriage grow stronger—and more consistent."

Then Dr. Lawrence offered counsel that startled James. "But don't make it your goal to get rid of mixed emotions altogether," she cautioned. "For one thing, you can't do it; your personality isn't built that way. For another, you shouldn't want to do it. Your mixed feelings actually are an advantage in many ways. For your assignment this week, I want you to think carefully about what benefits they may provide, and list as many as you can."

If you are as surprised as James was by Dr. Lawrence's counsel, you're not alone. Most people assume that fluctuating emotions are not our ideal mental state, and that our goal should be emotional consistency. A growing number of psychologists, though, regard a temperament such as James' as healthy, and see advantages to the ability to live with different feelings at the same time.

Psychologist Al Siebert extols this trait in his *The Survivor Personality*.[1] Siebert's concern in this exceptional book is to understand the personality features of people who are able to survive and thrive under life's most difficult conditions—including serious illness, financial collapse, natural disasters, war, concentration camps, and the like. He concludes that one of the most helpful traits for survival is the ability to live naturally with different emotions and different states of mind at the same time. This capacity enables you to be flexible, to adjust successfully to unwelcome circumstances, and to respond to the demands of emergencies. It also best positions you to recover from the ordeal and make a fresh start once it's over.

This ability to be in different worlds internally is a cherished gift, Siebert insists, not only in survival situations but in dealing with normal challenges of life. It helps us to live comfortably with imperfect situations and make the best of them, and aids us in many ways as we seek to accomplish goals and dreams.

"The protean self" is a term Siebert uses for this talent for emotional flexibility. It was coined by psychiatrist Robert Jay Lifton, in reference to Proteus, the Greek god of the sea, who changed his shape as circumstances required.

Historically, though, psychologists have not viewed the capacity for mixed emotions as a strength, but as a detriment to mental health, Siebert notes. The ideal has been emotional stability—to become a consistent optimist, for instance. A growing number now see the ideal differently—to be an optimist and a pessimist at the same time.

Seibert waits till his final chapter to introduce his most radical concept, perhaps fearing readers would turn him off if he mentioned it earlier. There he suggests that the ability to be at different places in one's thoughts and feelings is a "healthy schizophrenia." He doesn't mean that the delusional aspects of schizophrenia are desirable. But the inclination toward mixed emotions itself is life-giving when it's in right balance.

The Benefits of Emotional Flexibility

I find this notion redemptive, and highly compatible with Christian teaching. It is a comforting one as well. Most of us, if we're honest, experience fluctuating emotions and mood swings in many areas of life. We may be too quick to berate ourselves for this inclination and to see it purely as a curse on our life. We may wonder if we're mentally unbalanced.

In most cases the experience of mixed emotions doesn't signify mental illness. It's a healthy feature of our personality and a benefit to our life as God has designed it. The key is to understand specific ways this feature helps us, and then to harvest these advantages as fully as possible.

Scripture suggests at least four major ways that God builds into us the ability to live emotionally in two different worlds at once. Appreciating these points where he wants us to bend in different directions helps us see the value of a protean temperament, to our success in life and to our service for Christ.

1. The capacity for empathy. Empathy is the ability to put myself in another's shoes and identify with that person's feelings. No quality contributes more to my ability to share Christ's love with others, for empathy enables me to read someone's needs precisely, then to extend help they perceive as genuine.

Empathy enhances my own success immensely also, for it sharpens my judgment about how best to approach others for help. Siebert, in his book, lists empathy as one of the most important survival skills.

Yet the need for empathy presents me with an interesting

challenge, since different people in my life are usually at vastly different points of need. If I'm going to display empathy meaningfully to a variety of people, I'll need to be able to feel a variety of emotions at once. It's to this end that Paul counsels us, "Rejoice with those who rejoice, weep with those who weep" (Rom 12:15 RSV). Since it's often true that one person close to us is celebrating while another is grieving, we're expected to do nothing less than mourn and rejoice at the same time!

The ability to own different feelings simultaneously strengthens our potential for being empathetic, and for loving others effectively for Christ. The ongoing need we have for expressing empathy suggests that our goal shouldn't be to eliminate the experience of mixed emotions, but to channel the capacity for them in the best possible way.

2. Responding to life's roller-coaster nature. One of the most jubilant moments Evie and I enjoyed when our boys were young occurred one afternoon in May 1988, when Ben was in fifth grade. Arriving home from school that day, Ben announced he'd been elected president of Woodfield Elementary's student counsel. We were thrilled by his victory.

We hadn't celebrated it fifteen minutes when the phone rang. A friend was calling to inform us that she and her husband were divorcing. The couple were close friends of ours and role models to us as Christians. We were shocked by the news and deeply saddened, as we hadn't a clue there were problems in their marriage.

How often life presents us with this sort of roller coaster. A triumph in one area is followed by a setback in another.

The ability to live with different states of mind helps us to get through such episodes and not be derailed by them. At the best extreme (which we were far from in 1988), we're resilient, able to enjoy a success in spite of disappointments we're also experiencing, and able to continue pressing forward, leaving the past behind. If the mountaintop-to-the-valley experience goes with the territory in normal living, it's equally true that we often move quickly from the valley to the mountaintop when we keep our life in motion.

We see this vacillating nature of life often in the experiences of those in Scripture who lived courageously. The disciples in Acts who undertook evangelistic missions experienced constant shifts in public opinion. They were extolled as heroes one moment, derided as predators the next. After Paul and Barnabas healed a crippled man in Lystra, the citizens exclaimed, "The gods have come down to us in the likeness of men!" Even after Paul and Barnabas pleaded with the crowd not to deify them, "they scarcely restrained the people from offering sacrifice to them" (Acts 14:8-18 RSV).

These same people soon were willing to offer them *as* a sacrifice. In the next sentence Luke records, "But Jews came there from Antioch and Iconium; and having persuaded the people, they stoned Paul and dragged him out of the city, supposing that he was dead" (Acts 14:19 RSV).

On another occasion, islanders at Malta judged Paul a villain when a viper fastened to his hand. "This man must be a murderer; for though he escaped from the sea, the goddess Justice has not allowed him to live" (Acts 28:4). After a while, when Paul showed no ill effects, "they changed their minds and said he was a god" (Acts 28:6).

So life unfolds for each of us. Others' opinions of us change, and our fortunes rise and fall in many different ways. This oscillation can wear us down and diminish our desire to fight. However, God's objective through it all is to build into us a vibrant spirit of adventure—to the extent that we're stimulated by life's unpredictability rather than dismayed by it. When Jesus promised us abundant life (Jn 10:10), he was speaking of an adventuresome life, not one free of hills and valleys. We emphasize security far too much in our goals and expectations as Christians, when we ought be courting adventure more.

Appreciating the importance of adventure in God's plan for us helps us see the joy that is possible for us even when life takes on a "schizophrenic" quality. The ability to live in different worlds at once is at the heart of a healthy spirit of adventure, and the key to turning the page as God's plan for our life unfolds.

3. Embracing self-esteem and humility. God not only is building into us a greater instinct for adventure, but fashioning our self-image as well. He helps us, on the one hand, to think positively about our abilities and our potential for doing constructive things with our life. We each have an extraordinary need for such self-esteem. We need assurance we have gifts that are noteworthy, and opportunities to make an impact on human life that are significant.

We also have a substantial need for humility, and God is equally concerned with developing it in us. Without humility, we take our own importance too seriously. We elevate ourselves above the Lord and lose the incentive to grow. Humility in right measure keeps us on the growing edge and properly dependent upon the Lord.

No one short of a divine being could possibly have the wisdom to address both of these needs in us human creatures simultaneously. Yet God is constantly working in us, giving us appreciation of our gifts and vision for our life, while deepening our humility at the same time.

Peter's experience in the Gospels shows just how schizophrenic the process can seem. On one occasion, Jesus asks his disciples to identify who he is, and Peter responds, "You are the Messiah, the Son of the living God."

Jesus, ecstatic, commends Peter highly for this response, exclaiming,

> "Blessed are you, Simon son of Jonah, for this was not revealed to you by man, but by my Father in heaven. And I tell you that you are Peter, and on this rock I will build my church, and the gates of Hades will not overcome it. I will give you the keys of the kingdom of heaven; whatever you bind on earth will be bound in heaven, and whatever you loose on earth will be loosed in heaven." (Mt 16:13-20)

Jesus then begins to talk about his impending crucifixion, and Peter immediately rebukes him, declaring, "Never, Lord! . . .This shall never happen to you!"

Jesus just as abruptly rebukes Peter, retorting, "Get behind me, Satan! You are a stumbling block to me; you do not have in mind the concerns of God, but merely human concerns" (Mt 16:21-23).

Within a short time Peter is exalted by Jesus, then severely humbled. The extremes in this case are almost beyond belief: Jesus first extols Peter for a brilliant insight, calling him a "rock"—a courageous person—who will be a cornerstone in the emerging church; then Jesus chastises him for a foolish conclusion, labeling him Satan incarnate.

As we follow Peter throughout the Gospels and Acts, we

see this sequence repeated time and again: Jesus encourages him in one instance, reproves him in another. The implication is that this pattern will be ours as followers of Christ. If that thought seems unsettling, we should take heart in what Peter's example also teaches us—that through walking closely with Christ, we gain the ability to live comfortably with these different states of mind. Jesus developed this capacity in Peter during three years of discipleship, and the results were stunning. Following Jesus' ascension, Peter was able to assume leadership of the early church, and give inspired direction to its complex affairs.

We learn from Peter, then, that Christ builds protean qualities into us as we follow him, and that we are able to handle more challenging and fulfilling responsibilities as a result. Peter's example inspires us to take our relationship with Christ seriously—to give devoted time to prayer, to studying God's word, and to steps that best deepen the relationship for us personally. Through walking closely with Christ, we gain the treasured ability to live in different worlds at once, and the many benefits it confers.

4. Enjoying the blessings of life without allowing our well-being to depend upon any of them. God expects us to exult in the provisions he makes for our needs. At the same time, we're not to let our happiness hinge upon any of his temporal blessings.

Scripture expresses both of these needs in the strongest possible terms. Enjoyment isn't optional; we're *commanded* to rejoice in the bounty of life and to celebrate the accomplishments God makes possible for us. We're also warned severely against elevating any attraction to the status of an idol.

Again, we're expected to nurture inclinations that may seem

contradictory. Yet in truth, we need both of these qualities. Enjoying life contributes immensely to our health, vitality, productivity, relationships, and our ability to feel gratitude to God.

The problems that result when our love for some provision of life grows too strong are also substantial. A possession or relationship can take on so much importance that it consumes us; our identity is lost to it; our happiness rises or falls on how well it meets our expectations. Life loses its appeal in other areas, and if what we cherish is taken from us, our world collapses. Our neediness also works against us when we want something too much, for we're too quick to make compromises for the sake of it. When our affection for a person grows obsessive, for example, our neediness can kill the relationship. We lose the ability to treat the other person compassionately, for we're banking on her or him too greatly to meet our needs.

While we need, then, a strong inclination to enjoy the good things of life, we need some detachment from them as well. There are several secrets to living effectively in both these worlds at once—to review three principles we looked at in chapter seven for managing our desires:

• *Deepen your love for Christ.* As we've stressed, nothing helps us more to keep our desires and interests in right balance than a growing relationship with Christ. Through it we give him the fullest opportunity to inspire desires in us that move us in the best directions. A strong love for him also helps ensure that other affections will not take on more importance than they deserve.

When an attraction in our life has grown too strong, we usually address the problem best not by trying to tone down our desire, but by doing what we can to increase our love for Christ (C. S. Lewis).

• *Diversify.* We've stressed the importance of diversifying our interests as well. How often we learn this lesson from the stock market! Investing solely in one security is a dangerous strategy financially. The experts continually counsel us: Diversify your holdings. Don't put all your money into a single stock or type of investment.

The same principle applies to life. If we count on one relationship or interest in life to *be* life to us, we're in trouble. We do well to have a variety of friendships and not to expect any one person—not even our spouse—to provide all of our needs for friendship and intellectual stimulation. It's important as well to make new friendships as life moves on.

We should strive also to have more than one consuming interest. If we hit a dry spell in one, we can take refuge in another. Music and poetry gave David fresh heart for his leadership responsibilities. The craft of tent making played a similar role for Paul, Priscilla and Aquila, undoubtedly.

• *Be open to choices that reflect moderate desire, rather than extreme.* In areas of life where we may be prone to obsessive desire, we often do best to choose options where our affection is something less than volcanic. Many find their greatest happiness in a marriage in which romantic love is significant, but not mind-numbing. They are able to enjoy a life apart from the marriage, and have more to contribute to the relationship as a result. They are better able to focus on their partner's needs, to love that person, and less likely to destroy the marriage through excessive neediness.

Which brings us to why Dr. Lawrence counseled James as she did.

Dr. Lawrence didn't feel that James' mixed emotions signified his marriage was in trouble. Sarah is devoted to him and patient with his fluctuating feelings. James himself is a strong Christian, who loves Sarah compassionately, and is resolved to stay faithful.

What his mixed emotions demonstrate is that James isn't staking his happiness solely on the marriage. He has a life outside of it, and some important friendships and interests. The result is that he doesn't fall apart if Sarah isn't able to respond to his every need or if they experience conflict. Nor does he worry himself sick that she might leave him. He is naturally supportive of her and responsive to her needs, in part because he isn't living with outlandish expectations about her.

Dr. Lawrence recognized also that James cannot fully change the protean nature of his personality. He needs to begin by accepting it as a given in God's design of his life and to focus on its strengths. Over several sessions, Dr. Lawrence helped James appreciate many benefits of his temperament, and how it equips him to respond effectively to challenges.

A Gratifying Discovery

Many of us have a similar discovery to make. We've been berating ourselves for a characteristic that is actually a positive in God's intentions for our life. It can be stunning to realize how many ways a protean personality benefits us.

If you are one who often experiences mixed emotions, try a paradigm shift. Assume this tendency is a virtue, not a weakness. Take time to consider the benefits a protean temperament brings to your life, and note as many as you can. Realize you are better able to respond to certain demands of life than many others are.

Protean tendencies can cause us problems as well. If you are unable to make firm decisions or keep your commitments, or if you constantly feel miserable about the choices you make, then you are suffering too greatly from emotional swings. Counseling can help considerably in this case. With the help of the right "Dr. Lawrence," you can gain greater emotional stability and confidence about your decisions.

But begin with the premise that you are dealing with a strength, and need to modify its unhealthy extremes. Take heart that God fashioned your personality in the first place, and has an exceptional purpose for your life as you learn to channel your uniqueness in the best possible way. And there's no need for mixed emotions about that.

13

Self-Talk:
How Much Can We
Psych Ourselves Up?

FEW BIBLICAL INCIDENTS DO MORE to ignite my faith than the story about the woman with the hemorrhage. For twelve years she experienced the indescribable discomfort and embarrassment of a blood flow which no physician could heal. To add to her misery, she became financially destitute, bankrupt from her extensive medical expenses. Mark summarizes the woman's despair in a sentence: "She had suffered a great deal under the care of many doctors and had spent all she had, yet instead of getting better she grew worse" (Mk 5:26).

Finally, after this interminable search for help, she heard of Jesus and his exceptional power to heal. She pressed through a dense crowd to touch him, and at the instant when her hand made contact with his clothing she was cured.

This woman's example inspires me because I identify so easily with her humanity. She apparently was terribly frightened as she approached Jesus, for unlike most others in the Gospels who sought healing from him she attempted to do so unnoticed—by merely brushing the edge of his robe. Yet Jesus recognized instantly that healing power had escaped from him. When he asked who had touched him, "the woman, knowing what had happened to her, came and fell at his feet and, trembling with fear, told him the whole truth" (Mk 5:33).

Given her intense fear, it's all the more impressive that she found the resolve to approach Jesus for healing. It's this display of courage that impresses me most. I'm moved, too, by her incredible optimism: in spite of her constant experience of disappointment during more than a decade of seeking help from medical professionals, she still found it possible to believe that her health could be restored. What was the basis for her remarkable faith?

Matthew gives us a revealing insight when he notes that "she kept saying to herself, 'if I can only touch his coat, I will get well'" (Mt 9:21 Williams). She confronted her fears and doubts by telling herself repeatedly that she still had reason for hope—her past did not have to define her future.

Talking to Ourselves

Psychologists today would say that this woman benefited from positive "self-talk." The term has emerged in recent decades, both in pop psychology and in more serious circles as well, to describe an important part of our mechanism of thinking. Enthusiasts note that much—if not most—of our thinking is *verbalized.* If I wake up in the morning feeling depressed about the day ahead, for instance, I'm not just feeling some vague sense of despondency but am actually verbalizing a negative message to myself, such as, "I haven't had enough sleep. I won't be able to cope with the pressures ahead of me today, and I know my boss is going to give me too much to do." When we stop and look carefully at what is going on in our minds, we find that we're constantly talking to ourselves for good or ill during every conscious moment of life.

It is noted, too, that we can fall into certain patterns of negative self-talk early in life which if not checked continue with us for a lifetime. We are endlessly verbalizing messages to ourselves—consciously and unconsciously—about our prospects for success and happiness, and these mental memorandums dramatically affect our destiny. Persons with chronically low self-esteem, for instance, are constantly uttering statements of disapproval to themselves, such as, "I am no good. I make a mess of everything I try to do. I don't really have the right stuff to make friends or be successful, and even if I make the effort, no one is going to like me anyway."

Proponents of self-talk therapy argue that we can change virtually any behavior or thought pattern merely by altering the messages we speak to ourselves—"reprogramming the tracks," as it's called. To improve your self-image, for instance, simply make a habit of telling yourself, *I am someone of profound worth. I have the ability to make good friends and keep them, and the potential to make a significant mark in this world.* Or, if you're frightened about an upcoming job interview, calm your nerves and increase your prospects for success by saying repeatedly to yourself, *I have skills that are really needed by this company, and have good reason to hope the employer will quickly see this. I will be calm, articulate and friendly, and will present my case convincingly.*

The most provocative claim of self-talk devotees is that such efforts at constructive self-talk can quickly bring significant results, and that they hold the key to personal change—even to spiritual growth. In one of the most popular and influential books on the subject, *The Self-Talk Solution,* Shad Helmstetter regards positive self-talk as having a virtually hypnotic effect on our psyche. Simply change the way you talk to yourself in a given area, and surprising improvement will soon begin to take place, he insists. You can count on it.[1]

I Feel Good, I Feel Great . . .

Most of us react to such an idea with mixed emotions. We don't deny that much of our thinking is verbalized (how could anyone argue with that?), and we suspect that there probably are benefits to working on our self-talk. Yet we balk at the notion that self-talk is a cure-all for our problems or an instant guarantee of health, happiness and success. For one thing, it's hard to rid ourselves of the thought that our efforts at positive self-talk easily amount to a glorified sort of wishful thinking.

I've never forgotten an Archie comic strip I once read and its lighthearted jab at positive thinking. As I recall it, Jughead tells Archie that he fears he will fail at something he wants to do. Archie then gives Jughead some time-honored advice: "Tell yourself you can do it. Speak positive messages of success to yourself."

Jughead answers, "That won't work. I know what a liar I am!"

The insight of that simple four-frame comic strip is actually astounding, for it highlights a major reason why efforts at positive thinking so often backfire for the person with low self-confidence—the fact that she mistrusts her own judgment to begin with! While she has plenty of dreams of success and happiness, she assumes that these are largely fantasy. A more confident counselor may encourage a person to verbalize positive messages to himself. Yet it does little good to tell himself repeatedly, "You'll be successful in this job interview," if a louder voice underneath keeps announcing, "You usually fail—and this attempt to psych yourself up is a delusion." His chances for success are about as good as those of multiphobic Bob in the movie *What About Bob?*, who begins his daily routine and the movie chanting, "I feel good, I feel great, I feel wonderful," yet a moment later collapses in anxiety on the sidewalk.

Those with high self-esteem may benefit more readily from working on their self-talk. Yet they, too, likely discover that deeply ingrained thought patterns don't roll over and play dead as quickly as they would hope. It has been estimated that by the time we reach thirty years of age, our brain has been subjected to three trillion mental impressions. It takes more than a few casual efforts at positive self-talk to reprogram such tracks!

But then there is the example of the woman with the hemorrhage. She clearly benefited from telling herself that she would be healed if she touched Jesus' robe. Her self-talk seems to be the factor that nudged her beyond a considerable barrier of fear. Her step of courage so impressed Jesus that he declared, "Daughter, your faith has made you well"—one of the handful of instances in the Gospels where he praised someone's faith (Mk 5:34). Her inspiring example brings us back to the fact that the

Scriptures do see significance in the way we talk to ourselves.

What, then, are the real benefits of working on our self-talk, and what are the limitations?

Self-Talk in Scripture

To begin with—and for what it's worth—the Scriptures do give broad and perhaps surprising support to the fact that much of our thinking is verbalized. It's common, for instance, for biblical writers who are describing what an individual is thinking to use the words "said to himself." The phrase occurs frequently in Scripture, and clues us to numerous examples of verbalized thinking in the Bible. Most of these fall well short of the redemptive example of self-talk displayed by the woman with the hemorrhage; many, in fact, underline just how misguided self-talk can often be. For instance:

• Abraham fell facedown; he laughed and *said to himself,* "Will a son be born to a man a hundred years old? Will Sarah bear a child at the age of ninety?" (Gen 17:17)

• [The wicked man] *says to himself,* "God will never notice; he covers his face and never sees." (Ps 10:11)

• This is the carefree city that lived in safety. She *said to herself,* "I am, and there is none besides me." (Zeph 2:15)

• But suppose that servant is wicked and *says to himself,* "My master is staying away a long time," and he then begins to beat his fellow servants and to eat and drink with drunkards. (Mt 24:48-49)

Although these examples and many like them are negative, they do show Scripture respects the fact that we verbalize our thinking. They bring out, too, that our self-talk has more than a trivial effect upon our destiny.

There are also clear exhortations in Scripture to work on our self-talk. For example:

> • After the LORD your God has driven them out before you, *do not say to yourself,* "The LORD has brought me here to take possession of this land because of my righteousness." (Deut 9:4)

> • *Fix these words of mine in your hearts and minds;* tie them as symbols on your hands and bind them on your foreheads. Teach them to your children, talking about them when you sit at home and when you walk along the road, when you lie down and when you get up. (Deut 11:18-19)

These commands exhort us to constantly express to ourselves and others a grace-centered perspective on God. The fact that we're commanded to do this is encouraging to consider, for it indicates that God has given us the ability to do what is commanded. We *can* make improvements in our self-talk, in other words; Scripture *does* give us hope at this point.

No Quick Fix
Scripture, however, never comes close to suggesting that our lives can be dramatically improved or that deep-seated habits of thinking can be quickly changed merely by focusing on our self-talk alone. While the Bible is highly optimistic about posi-

tive change occurring in our lives, it cautions us against any attempt at a quick fix.

This comes across vividly in a discussion that Jesus had with his disciples about faith. On one occasion they came to him with an understandable request, "Increase our faith!" (Lk 17:5). Undoubtedly they were envious of Jesus' remarkable thought control. They wanted his uncanny capacity to believe without wavering that someone would be healed on command or—may we speculate?—that needs in their own lives would be instantly met. They wanted to get rid of all those negative messages inside their heads that kept saying, "This is impossible."

Jesus replied, "If you have faith as small as a mustard seed, you can say to this mulberry tree, 'Be uprooted and planted in the sea,' and it will obey you" (Lk 17:6). At first his reply seems puzzling, for he merely spoke to them of the challenge of increasing their faith, not about *how* to do it. He didn't seem to answer the question they asked. Yet I suspect Jesus realized that his disciples were looking for an easy shortcut to faith. He meant his response as a reality check, to jolt them into realizing the extreme difficulty of what they were asking. Even a very small *genuine* change in perspective is radical in nature and far-reaching in its effects. Or to say it conversely, it takes more than a few efforts at thought control or a wave of a spiritual magic wand to bring about an authentic change in outlook. This requires nothing less than a true inner transformation—and that takes time.

The point is pertinent to our discussion on self-talk, for our concern in improving our self-talk is, after all, how to increase our faith. Here we're reminded that our greatest faith need is not to become momentarily psyched up, but to experience a thoroughgoing change in perspective. We need to become *thoroughly persuaded* of Christ's vibrant outlook on our life, not just temporarily enthused about it.

This brings us back, then, to the question of how such a radical change in perspective can come about.

Temporary Elation vs. True Transformation

A variety of steps may be helpful, including regular worship, careful study of Scripture, seeking the support and encouragement of others—even professional counseling if needed. Yet over the long haul, I do not believe any activity helps us more to gain an outlook of faith than times of personal meditation. By "meditation" I don't mean incantations or lotus postures but simply a time of quiet pondering, when we reflect on our life and on God, and when we give Christ an ample opportunity to get our ear—the sort of practice I recommended in chapter one for daily managing our emotions. It's through such periods that the most substantial and lasting changes in perspective are likely to occur.

This is the lesson we learn from Psalm 73. The writer of that psalm was overwhelmed with bitterness, as he compared his lot in life to that of certain unscrupulous individuals he knew who were outrageously successful. He concluded that God had dealt him a low blow. Yet through a period of silent reflection he began to recognize the fate of these fraudulent individuals more clearly, and to view his own life more optimistically. He moved beyond his acid spirit of comparison to a more vibrant outlook on God—and on his own life as well.

For him, the change in perspective occurred in the reverent

stillness of a sanctuary. There was nothing magic about that location, for Moses had similar experiences on a mountain, Jesus in a garden, while John the Baptist and Paul benefited from the peaceful environment of the desert. The location is not the critical factor, as Jesus indicated when he suggested that we pray in a "closet" (Mt 6:6 KJV). The important matter is simply to arrange for a reasonable period of quiet, and to choose a location that will enhance it.

Again, I believe that each of us will benefit greatly from spending at least a few minutes daily in quiet reflection. During this period we should bring to the surface those areas of our life where we feel frustrated or discouraged. We should consider the hidden benefits these situations may actually have for us, and leisurely explore possible solutions and reasons for hope. We should ponder the biblical teaching on Christ's grace and provision in our lives, and consider what relation this teaching has to the challenges we're facing. God, as we've stressed, has made our minds amazingly resilient, incredibly capable of regaining a sense of hope and generating optimistic solutions. Yet for this to happen, we have to allow adequate opportunity for the Holy Spirit to influence us and renew within us the mind of Christ. This means, especially, the need for times of quiet.

As we stressed in chapter one, we should also reflect on how we're doing in managing our feelings—how the past day has gone, and how we can best prepare for the emotional challenges of the current day. Ideally, this meditation should occur during a regular devotional time, when we pray and study Scripture as well as take time to reflect. Unfortunately, our "quiet" times too often become cluttered with busy routines—prayer lists, study requirements and other rituals, which can become a subtle effort to court God's favor through our spirituality. While these practices can be valuable, we must remember that the ultimate purpose of a devotional time is to give praise to Christ and to gain his perspective and encouragement for our day. George Muller expressed it well when he said, "I consider it my first business of the day to get my heart happy in the Lord." Each of us needs to experiment to find out what approach will best accomplish that purpose. Most of us will find that a period of quiet, uncluttered reflection will be immensely helpful, even if it means discarding some of the busy routine of our devotional time.

Early in his career, Christian psychiatrist Paul Tournier decided to devote an hour daily to this sort of meditation. His many books bustle with stories of how this practice benefited both himself and his patients. Though setting this hour aside meant cutting back on other responsibilities, Tournier insisted that the tradeoff was more than worth it.

An hour daily of personal meditation will be too much for many of us. Yet each of us will find that *some* time given each day to such reflection will benefit us and be worth the exchange of time involved. From time to time, we will also find that a personal retreat or special extended period of prayer and reflection will help greatly to clarify things and rekindle our faith.

More than Just Talk
Let's return to the example of the woman with the hemorrhage. I believe that her extraordinary faith sprang not merely from efforts to psych herself up, but from a deep conviction about the grace and goodness of God. In spite of her extreme suffering, she was profoundly persuaded that God desired the very

best for her, and that she had considerable reason for hope. Her illness, in fact, may well have provided the enforced solitude for her to think things through to this point. As she ventured forth to seek healing from Jesus, she was dreadfully frightened—and naturally so, for she had plenty of inertia to overcome, the reactions of unsympathetic people to face, and plenty of disheartening thoughts to deal with. In light of this, telling herself again and again that Jesus would heal her did prove helpful—but in reality *she was simply reminding herself of what she already knew.*

Here we finally come to the point of saying what is the real benefit of working on our self-talk. *Self-talk has maintenance value for us.* It's a way of bringing ourselves back to points of conviction we've already reached during times of quiet reflection before the Lord, especially as the more frantic pace of life drowns them out. It's a way of combating fears that all too naturally crop up, even once we become convinced of what God wants us to do. When used in healthy balance with times of prayer and meditation, it can truly aid us in practicing the presence of the Lord.

You and I need to keep telling ourselves that.

14

Listening to God:
Why It Helps
To Be Moving

IN HIS *CHRONICLES, VOLUME ONE*, Bob Dylan reflects on the setting he believes best enables him and others to compose music. It is one, he explains, that is anything but stationary: "You can write a song anywhere, in a railroad compartment, on a boat, on horseback—it helps to be moving." He adds, "Sometimes people who have the greatest talent for writing songs never write any because they are not moving."[1]

Dylan makes this observation—that musical inspiration best comes when one is "moving"—deep into his book, just in passing, and doesn't elaborate further. Yet it gripped my interest, and on a broader level, for I've often sensed that our most important insights about life and personal challenges tend to come when we're in motion. Think about your own experience: Re-call those welcome times when the answer to a pressing deci-sion or problem suddenly became clear. I will guess the majority of them occurred when you were on a trip, or running an errand, or taking a walk. It's less likely they happened when you were stationary—sitting at home, or busy with your normal routine at work.

I've long been intrigued that many of the most important epiphanies of the great heroes of Scripture occurred when they were traveling. The stunning revelations Abraham experienced, for instance—when God revealed that he would be the father of many nations—took place only after he left his hometown of Haran and "went out, not knowing whither he went" (Heb 11:8 KJV).

Or consider Jacob's experience. For long periods of his life, he was stuck in one place—first Canaan, then Haran for twenty years, then Canaan again for a lengthy period until, in old age, he moved to Egypt. He grew increasingly sedentary as life moved on, and, it would appear, increasingly depressed. Scrip-ture, though, notes six instances when God gave Jacob a cher-ished, direct revelation. Four occurred at those rare times when Jacob was traveling and moving from one location to another (Gen 28:10-22; 32:22-30; 35:9-15; 46:1-4); he had a dramatic encounter with God in each case, and received profound assur-ance of God's blessing and protection.

On Jacob's other two occasions of direct revelation, God told him that he *should* travel. God advised him to move from Haran back to Canaan in one case (Gen 31:3, 10-13), and then later, instructed him to visit Bethel, where Jacob had previously encountered God (Gen 35:1). In both of these instances, it's likely that Jacob was seriously considering making the trip God told him to undertake. The *anticipation* of traveling, then, may have prepared him psychologically for the revelation he received.

And—Genesis notes a further occasion when angels appeared to Jacob, though no mention is made of them or of God's speaking to Jacob in this case (Gen 32:1-2). Yet Jacob was clearly elated by this encounter, and took great reassurance from it. It also occurred when he was . . . *traveling!*—on his trip from Haran back home to Canaan. "Jacob . . . went on his way, and the angels of God met him. When Jacob saw them, he said, 'This is the camp of God!' So he named that place Mahanaim."

We find many examples like these of Abraham and Jacob throughout Scripture, where individuals received vital guidance or reassurance from God while they were either on a trip or at its destination.

The Insight of Proverbs

Of even greater interest are two passages in the book of Proverbs. Proverbs speaks extensively about the wisdom God gives us for resolving decisions and problems, and of how critical it is for us to seek it. The individual proverbs note many practical steps we can take to gain wisdom, and often compare wise actions with foolish ones. Two passages in Proverbs, though, advise us about *the setting* in which we're most likely to gain wise insight. And in both cases, we're told that it's one in which we're *on the go:*

> Wisdom cries aloud in the street; in the markets she raises her voice; on the top of the walls she cries out; at the entrance of the city gates she speaks . . . . (Prov 1:20-21 RSV)

Does not wisdom call? Does not understanding raise her voice? On the heights beside the way, in the paths she takes her stand; beside the gates in front of the town, at the entrance of the portals she cries aloud .... (Prov 8:1-3 RSV)

Wisdom is personified in these passages (and here only in Proverbs)—as a voice offering insight to the receptive person. Does this mean we are likely to hear an audible voice responding if we ask for God's guidance? I doubt it. Nowhere in the rest of Proverbs, or anywhere else in Scripture, is it taught that we should expect to hear a supernatural voice revealing God's will. The continual message of Proverbs is that wisdom comes from our diligent, practical effort to attain it.

Yet we also enjoy harvest experiences in seeking wisdom, when we suddenly have a burst of wise insight, and see the answer to a problem or decision that has confounded us. These moments can come with such great impact that we feel as though we've experienced a divine revelation. We may be inclined to say that God has spoken to us at such times. Undoubtedly, it's this sort of experience that the writer has in mind in these passages, when he mentions wisdom speaking and raising her voice.

What the writer *is* clearly saying is that these episodes of enlightenment will most likely take place when we're on trips or errands. We might expect to read the opposite: that they will occur when we're sitting quietly at home thinking or praying. But while Scripture doesn't rule out that possibility, these passages suggest that our most profound insights will probably come when we're away from home and on our way somewhere.

What this "being on our way" involves is the most fascinating part. That it may include major travel is evident when the writer refers to wisdom speaking "on the heights beside the way" and "at the crossroads." But he also mentions wisdom speaking "in the markets," "at the head of the noisy streets," and "at the entrance of the city gates." We may enjoy a blessed moment of enlightenment, in other words, on our *short* trips—such as for shopping or social purposes! On these excursions, or at their destinations, we're in a special position to experience a personal epiphany.

The fact that moving about in our normal business of the day can boost our receptivity to God's wisdom is extraordinarily encouraging. It brings purpose to the mundane traveling we constantly have to do, and a basis for anticipating something special happening on such trips. It just might be that on a drive to the mall or the doctor's office we suddenly see a matter clearly that's been baffling us.

These passages from Proverbs even lead us to believe that God might surprise us with life-changing guidance when we're—heaven forbid—*commuting*. The reference to wisdom speaking in the "noisy streets" seems even more divinely inspired for our own time than for when the passage was written!

Why It Helps to Be in Motion

The writer of these proverbs doesn't tell us why we can be so open to enlightenment when we're "out and about," but I suspect that several reasons contribute. For one, when we're on a trip or an errand to a destination we want to reach, we tend to be more optimistic than usual. We're also more relaxed and more right-brain oriented. In these states, our mind is more likely to think creatively, and to make positive connections between the myriad of details we're mulling. The solution to a difficult decision or problem may suddenly become plain.

Usually, too, we're more physically invigorated when we're traveling than when we're sitting still at home or at the office. This was certainly true for people in biblical times, who for transportation relied on walking or bumpy rides on horses, mules, or camels. With better circulation comes better thinking.

And, as we move along on a trip, our eyes are continually exposed to new sights. This rapid change in visual detail can stimulate our mind to process other information more quickly and effectively.

Perhaps most important—and most simply—traveling breaks the inertia for us. If we're stuck and unable to resolve a problem or decision, anything we do to get our body moving helps to get our mind moving as well.

It's hard to exaggerate the importance that traveling has played in my own experience of Christ's guidance. My decision to launch Sons of Thunder, and the solution to some major problems related to doing it, came during a visit to Rehoboth Beach in summer 1966, when I was driving the ocean highway between Rehoboth and Ocean City, Maryland. The conclusion to ask Evie Kirkland to marry me was reached while I was driving from the Maryland town of Mt. Airy to Damascus, where we now live. I discovered the home we presently live in while on a leisurely drive in upper Montgomery County, Maryland, to pray about the matter of finding a new home. Countless ideas for writing have come while I'm driving as well. My mind always seems to work better then, and my heart seems more receptive to the Lord's inspiration.

Motion vs. Stillness

This isn't to say that God only guides us when we're in motion. There is a vital place for stillness in the Christian life. Jesus instructed his disciples, "when you pray, go into your room and shut the door and pray to your Father who is in secret" (Matt 6:5). He encouraged them to seek this privacy, in part, to avoid prideful public displays of devotion, but also, I'm sure, to remove distractions. We can have too much movement in our life—to say the least. The pace of life is so frantic for some of us, that we need to heed the timeless counsel of Psalm 46:10: "Be still and know that I am God."

Yet what contributes to stillness differs greatly for each of us. Jesus himself often retreated to the Garden of Gethsemane for meditation, where he may well have spent more time walking than sitting. While I do plenty of praying at home, I have to be walking around the house to do it; I can't pray sitting for long without losing my focus or dozing off.

One highly respected Christian leader, Dr. Richard Halverson, confessed to me that chaos and distractions actually helped him focus better. He could just as easily have a deep devotional time sitting in a subway station as in his home study.

Each of us has a need to find the right balance between stillness and movement in our life, and to find what circumstances best help us to enjoy peaceful reflection and to focus effectively in prayer.

If we've been Christian for any time, though, we've heard plenty of emphasis on the importance of being quiet and still before the Lord. We understand quite well our need to do this. Yet we've probably heard little or no stress on the spiritual value of being on the go. The fact that being in motion can boost our receptivity to God is unspeakably encouraging, for the simple reason that so much of our life, by default, involves being in transit.

Practical Implications

Most of us can learn to benefit much more than we do from this remarkable life principle. Here are several steps that can help:

• If your life involves plenty of traveling, make a practice of reminding yourself before each trip, whether short or long, that being on the road may help you better understand God's guidance for some important matter. If there's a decision you're facing, or a problem you're trying to solve, pray at least briefly that God will enlighten you on this matter while you travel. Then take some time while you're on your way to pray or just reflect; if you're driving, turn off the radio, CD player and cell phone for at least part of the trip. Enjoy the quiet, and be open to inspiration. Not every trip will bring the epiphany of a lifetime, to be sure, and many will pass without dramatic enlightenment. But on occasion, a welcome insight will emerge that makes the whole effort worthwhile.

• Commuting can aid our spiritual openness in the same ways other travel does. I say *can*, for commuting involves a different routine for each of us. You are more likely to be in the mood for inspiration if your trip to work is a quiet train ride or a pleasant country drive, than if you're sitting in a carpool van with five other people and talk radio blaring. And if aggravating traffic tie-ups are common in your drive to work, you'll find it harder to maintain a devotional spirit.

But—simply be open. When you set forth on your commute to work, you're leaving home, breaking the inertia, and getting yourself on the move. You're doing things that may position you better to listen to God. Be open to his surprising you with special insight as you commute, and expect the best in your trips to and from work.

• If your life has grown—to be honest—too sedentary, do what you can to put more movement into it. Remember the potential spiritual value of any traveling you do, including simple jaunts like shopping trips. Take a leisurely drive for the purpose of praying, reflecting, and seeking a better understanding of God's direction. Or take a walk or bike ride for the same purpose.

But what if you're disabled and have limited ability to get around? You are not at a disadvantage in listening to God in this case—most definitely not. God works with each of us in light of our capabilities, and meets us where we are (that is the message of Christ's incarnation, that God comes to us *where we are!*). What mobility you do have will work for you, so make the best of it. And take heart that God will compensate for your disability in numerous ways, including his means of guiding you.

• A personal retreat can be an outstanding way to reap the very best spiritual benefits of traveling and escaping life's normal distractions. At least once a year, plan a time—an afternoon, a day or two, or longer—for concentrating exclusively on your relationship with Christ and his guidance for you. Spend your personal retreat in a quiet setting away from home, where you are not likely to be interrupted. And remember that your trip to and from your retreat destination is part of the adventure; it may even be the time when your most treasured insights come!

• Finally, exercise can provide us some of the same benefits for spiritual inspiration that traveling often does. Exercise—to say the obvious—gets our blood circulating, breaks the inertia and gets us moving. And, as we've noted, travel in biblical times usually involved some form of exertion.

I recently read a stunning account of how Nikola Tesla invented the AC induction engine. As a young Serbian student, Tesla had wrestled with the concept of this motor for several years while studying in Paris. But he couldn't solve the technical problems that had long confounded other inventors, and a professor publicly ridiculed him for even imagining such an engine could be developed. Overworked and exhausted, Tesla suffered a nervous breakdown. A friend then convinced Tesla to begin exercising for the health benefits. While Tesla and his friend were on their workout routine one afternoon, they wandered into a city park; at that point, the engine's design suddenly became crystal clear to Tesla.

"I drew with a stick in the sand. . . . The images I saw were wonderfully sharp and clear and had the solidity of metal and stone, so much that I told [my friend], 'See my motor here; watch me reverse it.' I cannot begin to describe my emotions."[2]

It wasn't until about a decade later that Tesla finally gained the financial backing and resources to build his motor. Until then, he merely carried its design in his mind and never wrote it down, unflinchingly convinced it would work. His conviction proved bulletproof accurate: once built, his motor performed flawlessly. During his lifetime, Tesla saw it become accepted as the standard for electric motors throughout the world. It vastly improved production for every major industry, and alleviated the burdens of countless people in their daily tasks—fulfilling Tesla's primary hope for this invention. Today, if you've eaten food from your refrigerator, used an electric shaver, enjoyed the benefits of air-conditioning, driven your car, or filled a glass with water simply by turning on a faucet, you've benefited profoundly from the epiphany of a young student exercising in a Paris park on a blustery February afternoon in 1882.

I mention Tesla's experience because exercising seems to have given him an edge that helped him achieve the creative inspiration of a lifetime. His was an astounding experience, I believe, of divine inspiration—given to one who, as a near-candidate for the priesthood, certainly understood it and was undoubtedly seeking it.

Guidance as a Moving Experience

I'm not suggesting that exercise or travel will necessarily open any of us to such an insight that changes the world. But it may open us more fully to inspiration from God that changes our life, or that helps us realize our potential in important ways. If you are looking forward to a vacation trip anytime soon, anticipate it not only as a time of leisure, but as one when God may break through with guidance you greatly need. And make a habit of seeing daily travel and exercise as an opportunity to think more clearly, with the mind of Christ, about your life.

And, as you study Scripture, be alert to the many examples of those who received critical inspiration from the Lord while they were on the move. We see time and again how simply getting ourselves in motion can make all the difference.

15

Conclusion

HALFWAY THROUGH AN intensive graduate program, I lost my zeal. My pastoral heartstrings tugged at me; I wanted to get out of academia and back into people-centered ministry. I came close to quitting.

On Evie's advice I decided to seek counsel from the dean of students. When I walked into his office the next morning, he received me warmly and spoke with me at length, even though I hadn't made an appointment. After I explained my dilemma, he offered some simple advice: I needed to be willing to make some tradeoffs. It was a reasonable tradeoff, he said, to spend some "dry time" in exchange for the creative period that I'd already enjoyed. Besides, I would soon finish the program and could then begin to enjoy its benefits. When all of the angles were considered, the tradeoffs were certainly more than worth it.

As basic as this advice was, it hit a receptive chord with me.

It was the right thought at the right time and gave me fresh heart. Once it dawned on me that it was okay to make some tradeoffs in order to complete the program, I felt comfortable doing so. By the end of our meeting my motivation had begun to return.

I'm now eternally grateful to this man for his advice and encouragement. Staying with the program gave me the background to write my first book, and the degree has opened numerous doors for ministry. In this case God used a man—one individual—to keep me from a regrettable course of action. Were it not for his counsel, I likely would have bailed out.

This experience, which I detail in *The Yes Anxiety*, also showed me that I didn't understand my temperament well. I was studying the will of God at Fuller Theological Seminary, and had begun the program eager to make some contribution on the topic. But at this midpoint, I assumed my motivation had permanently waned, and that I didn't have the zeal to complete the course of study. Yet my passion not only bounced back enough to finish, but then to write a book on God's guidance, and then to launch a thirty-year teaching ministry where about half my focus was on this topic. I shudder to think how much I would have missed, and how greatly I would have diminished my potential to help others, by caving in to those feelings of the moment—which I was only too close to doing.

In *Emotional Intelligence*, Daniel Goleman laments the extreme focus in America upon educating the left brain to the exclusion of the right. Our academic process produces many who are brilliant in certain fields of knowledge but who don't understand or manage their feelings well. In my own case, I had sat through more than twenty years of class time by now and was in a doctoral program. Yet at no point in this extensive scholastic odyssey had anyone ever taught me how to handle my feelings. Never had anyone taught me about *motivation*, and the basic fact that my enthusiasm for an academic goal or career might vacillate, even when the path is fully right for me. The results could have been tragic, apart from the wise counsel and encouragement the dean of students gave me that morning.

That experience and certain others ignited in me a since-lifetime interest in how our self-understanding affects our happiness, success and relationship with Christ. And this concern, along with knowing God's will, has been a central focus of my teaching and writing for the past several decades. I hope that this book has awakened in you a similar interest in better understanding your temperament and managing your emotions—in short, in this grand area Goleman terms emotional intelligence. And I hope it spurs you to make growing wise emotionally a lifestyle and ongoing lifetime goal. We've looked at some critical areas related to emotional intelligence in this book, and if you'll simply put the practical counsel in these pages into action, it can make a huge difference in both your quality of life and what you accomplish.

Besides the areas we've covered, there are many others related to emotional intelligence that you can profit from studying. I encourage you especially to look for books by Christian authors that focus on the integration of psychology and spirituality. I've authored several others myself, including *One of a Kind: A Biblical View of Self-Acceptance; Overcoming Shyness; The Yes Anxiety: Taming the Fear of Commitment,* and *Faith and Optimism: Positive Expectation in the Christian Life.* There are, of course, countless other good books on psychological topics out there by Christian writers, and Amazon and other Internet sites make it exquisitely easy to search for them. And practical "self-help" books on these subjects, like Goleman's *Emotional Intelligence* and others I've cited in this book, can also be of tremendous value to you as a Christian, if you read them thoughtfully, with an eye toward what agrees with biblical teaching.

Finally, you may find it helpful in capping off this present study to go back and review chapter one. The practical counsel in that chapter alone, if you put it into practice, will take you a significant distance toward managing your emotions successfully and reaping the considerable benefits. I urge you especially, if you haven't yet, to begin including a time for reflecting on your emotional life into your daily schedule, along the lines I suggest in that chapter. Incorporate it into your devotional time, or use it as a basis for starting one.

I wish you God's very best as you seek to live a life that's more enlightened emotionally, and I sincerely hope the reflections in this book will prove helpful to you in this journey. When David spoke of being "fearfully and wonderfully made" by God (Psalm 139:14 KJV), he undoubtedly had in mind the dangers his emotions posed (the fearfully-made part) and well as their potential for bringing great blessing to him and others (the wonderfully-made part). The dynamic tension between these extremes clearly sparked in David a great sense of adventure. May this sense of adventure be yours also, as you seek to grow wiser emotionally and to live your life more wholeheartedly for Christ. May you find yourself daily experiencing his joy in greater measure, along with greater confidence of his guidance, and greater purpose in striving to realize the unique potential he has given you. Bon adventure, my friend!!!

Notes

Chapter 1: Growing Wise Emotionally
[1]Daniel Goleman, *Emotional Intelligence: Why It Can Matter More Than IQ* (New York: Bantam Books, 1995).

Chapter 2: Reshaping Assumptions That Shape Our Life
[1]Ellen J. Langer, *Mindfulness* (Perseus Books, Cambridge, Massachusetts, 1989).

Chapter 3: Embracing Optimism
[1]David Richo, Ph.D., *Unexpected Miracles: The Gift of Synchronicity and How to Open It* (New York: Crossroad Publishing, 1998), p. 30.
[2]Seligman explains this perspective in detail in his book: Martin E. P. Seligman, Ph.D., *Learned Optimism: How to Change Your Mind and Your Life* (New York: A. A. Knopf, 1991; and New York: Pocket Books, 1992).

Chapter 5: Is Anger a Sin?
[1]Vernon Grounds, *Emotional Problems and the Gospel* (Grand Rapids, Mi.: Zondervan Publishing House, 1976), p. 56.

Chapter 6: If I Don't Express My Anger Will I Blow Up?
[1]Dale Carnegie, *How to Win Friends and Influence People,* Revised Edition (New York: Pocket Books, 1981) pp. 10-11.
[2]Carol Tavris, *Anger: The Misunderstood Emotion* (New York: Touchstone Books, 1982).

Chapter 7: Pearls of Too Great a Price?
[1]John Steinbeck, *The Pearl* (New York: Penguin Books, 1976), p. 18.
[2]Ibid., p. 20.
[3]Herb Cohen, *You Can Negotiate Anything* (New York: Bantam Books, 1980).

Chapter 8: Welcome Guidance from Unwelcome Circumstances
[2]W. Clement Stone, *The Success System That Never Fails* (New York: Prentice Hall, 1962).

Chapter 9: The Peril of Despair
[1]Robert M. Bramson, Ph.D., *Coping with Difficult People* (New York: Dell Publishing, 1981) pp. 102-03.
[2]Steve Simms, *Mindrobics: How to Be Happy the Rest of Your Life* (Brentwood, Tennessee: Attitude-Lifter Enterprises, 1995).

Chapter 12: The Power of Resilience
[1]Al Siebert, Ph.D., *The Survivor Personality: Why Some People*

Are Stronger, Smarter, and More Skillful at Handling Life's Difficulties . . . and How You Can Be, Too (New York: A Perigee Book, 1996).

Chapter 13: Self-Talk: How Much Can We Psych Ourselves Up?
[1]Shad Helmstetter, *The Self-Talk Solution: Take Control of Your Life—With the Self-Management Program for Success!* (New York: Pocket Books, 1988).

Chapter 14: Listening to God: Why It Helps to Be Moving
[1]Bob Dylan, *Chronicles, Volume One* (New York: Simon & Shuster, 2004) p. 164.
[2]Jill Jonnes, *Empires of Light: Edison, Tesla, Westinghouse, and the Race to Electrify the World* (New York: Random House, 2003), pp. 92-93.

About the Author

Blaine Smith, a Presbyterian pastor, spent 30 years as director of Nehemiah Ministries, Inc., a resource ministry based in the Washington, D.C. area. He retired the organization in 2009, but continues to use the name Nehemiah Ministries for free-lance work.

His career has included giving seminars and lectures, speaking at conferences, counseling, and writing. He is author of ten books, including *Marry a Friend*, *Knowing God's Will* (original and revised editions), *Should I Get Married?* (original and revised editions), *The Yes Anxiety*, *Overcoming Shyness*, *Faith and Optimism* (originally *The Optimism Factor)*, *One of a Kind*, *Reach Beyond Your Grasp*, and *Emotional Intelligence for Christians*, as well as numerous articles. These books have been published in more than thirty English language and international editions. He is also lecturer for *Guidance By The Book*, a home study course with audio cassettes produced by the Christian

Broadcasting Network as part of their *Living By The Book* series.

Blaine served previously as founder/director of the Sons of Thunder, believed by many to be America's first active Christian rock band, and as assistant pastor of Memorial Presbyterian Church in St. Louis. He is an avid guitarist, and currently performs with the Newports, an oldies band.

Blaine is a graduate of Georgetown University, and also holds a Master of Divinity from Wesley Theological Seminary and a Doctor of Ministry from Fuller Theological Seminary. He and Evie live in Gaithersburg, Maryland. They've been married since 1973, and have two grown sons, Benjamin and Nathan. Ben and his wife Lorinda have two children, Jackson Olen (2009) and Marlena Mae (2012).

Blaine also authors a twice-monthly online newsletter, *Nehemiah Notes*, featuring a practical article on the Christian faith, posted on his ministry website and available by e-mail for free. You may e-mail Blaine at mbs@nehemiahministries.com.

Made in the USA
Middletown, DE
26 January 2022

59641944R00113